XERXES DOMAIN

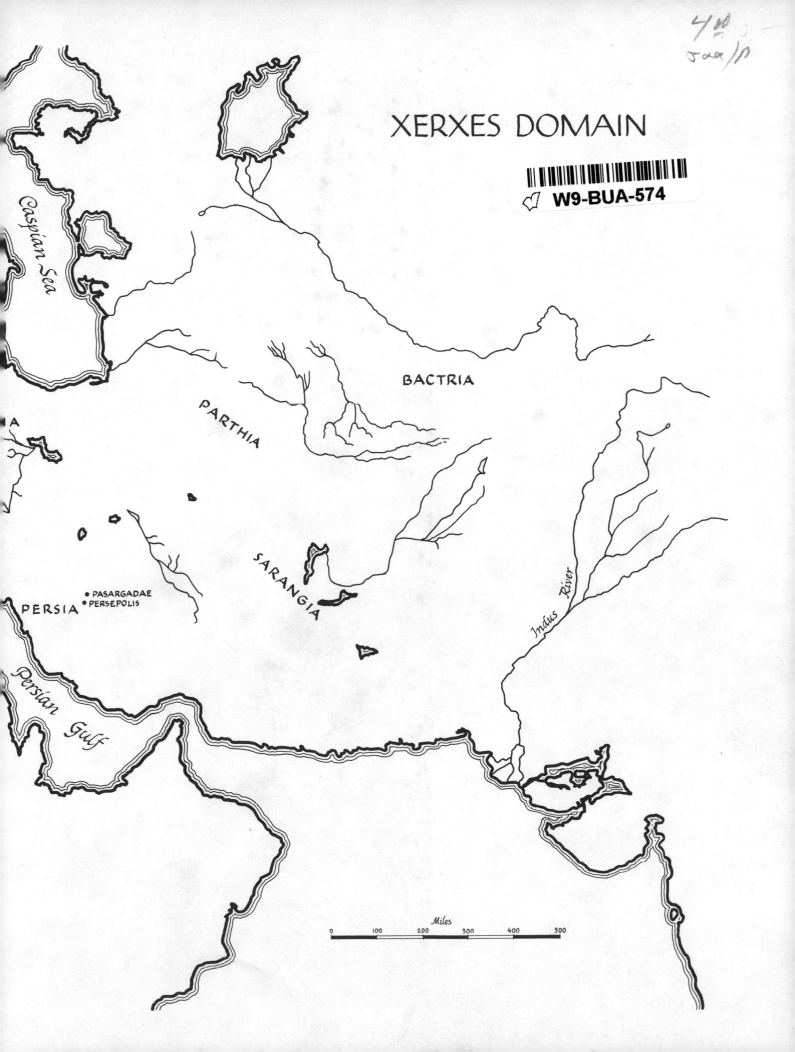

Caspian Sea

BACTRIA

PARTHIA

SARANGIA

Indus River

PERSIA

• PASARGADAE
• PERSEPOLIS

Persian Gulf

Miles
0   100   200   300   400   500

Preface by HOMER A. THOMPSON

Translation by Aubrey de Sélincourt

DEMOCRACY'S FIRST STRUGGLE

HERODOTUS' HISTORIES

Edited and with photographs by

JOSEPH C. FARBER

1975

BARRE PUBLISHING

BARRE, MASSACHUSETTS

DISTRIBUTED BY Crown Publishers, INC., NEW YORK

TO MY FRIEND THE LATE
ALDEN P. JOHNSON

ILLUSTRATIONS:
Page i, *Herodotus' podium at Olympia*
Title page, *Broken gold Persian dagger*

Maps by Karl Rueckert

Printed in the United States of America
Library of Congress Cataloging in Publication Data
Herodotus.
    Democracy's first struggle.
    Selections from the Histories.
    1. History, Ancient. I. Farber, Joseph C.,
1903–   II. De Sélincourt, Aubrey, 1894–1962.
III. Title.
D.58.H335 1975   930   72-95110
ISBN 0-517-52094-X

Published simultaneously in Canada by
General Publishing Company Limited
Inquiries should be addressed to Crown Publishers, Inc.
419 Park Avenue South, New York, N.Y. 10016
First edition

Contents

ACKNOWLEDGMENTS   vi

PREFACE   vii

Ancient Kings of Asia   1

Travels in Egypt   11

Darius Becomes King   47

The Battle at Marathon   55

Xerxes Plans to Conquer Greece   69

Battles of Thermopylae and Artemisium   91

Salamis   109

Plataea   131

APPENDIX   146

LOCATION OF PHOTOGRAPHS   147

INDEX   149

Acknowledgments

Without the encouragement of Professor Homer A. Thompson, Dr. Helen Bacon, Mr. Leon Pomerance and Mrs. Harriet Pomerance, this book would have been just an idea.

Throughout the work many people helped greatly, too many for this page to list. At the beginning Dr. Bernard Bothmer and Dr. Seth Benardette helped to give direction to the project. In Greece Dr. Eugene Vanderpool made the battles, particularly Marathon, seem as though they had just happened. Dr. Labib Habichi opened my eyes to ancient Egypt, and helped me understand what Herodotus saw. The photographs giving the Persian background are the result of ideas and assistance from Dr. Vaughn E. Crawford.

The kind understanding of Ronald Johnson, publisher, and Klaus Gemming, the designer, has been invaluable.

My wife, Caroline, visualized many of the scenes and offered innumerable constructive suggestions and criticism.

· · ·

Permission by the following to make photographs is greatly appreciated:

The Acropolis Museum (AM), The Agora Museum (AGM), The American Numismatic Society (ANS), The American School of Classical Studies (Athens) (ASCS), The Boston Museum of Fine Arts (BMFA), The Delphi Museum (DM), The Egyptian Antiquity Service (EAS), The Egyptian Museum (Cairo) (EM), The Greek Department of Antiquities, The Metropolitan Museum of Art (MM), The National Museum (Athens) (NM), The Olympia Museum (OM), and The Sparta Museum (SM).

HERODOTUS was born in 484 B.C. or thereabouts—early, that is, in the long struggle between Greeks and Persians that was to be the theme of his lifework. His birthplace, the old Greek city of Halicarnassus, modern Bodrum, on the coast of Asia Minor, lay on the borderline between the Greek and the Persian worlds; at the time of his birth it had been for many years under Persian suzerainty. Political troubles drove him at an early age to leave home and take refuge on the nearby island of Samos. In middle age he joined the colony of Thurii founded by Athens in south Italy in 444/3 B.C. In the marketplace of that city was shown his tomb inscribed with the epigram: "This dust covers the body of Herodotus, son of Lyxes, master of old Ionic history. Born in a land of Dorian men he fled from their intolerable accusations and made Thurii his homeland." His death occurred soon after 430 B.C. near the beginning of the Pelopennesian War that was to provide a theme for his younger contemporary, Thucydides, his junior by some thirty years.

This virtually exhausts the information we have about Herodotus' career. The intervening years are obscure, but they appear to have been full of travel. References in his own writings attest visits to various cities of Asia Minor and inland as far as Sardis, to the Aegean islands, to the Peloponnese, central and northern Greece, to the Black Sea as far as the Crimea. Eastward he had visited Cyprus, the coast of Phoenicia and inland to the Euphrates and Babylon. The homeland of the Persians he seems to have known only by hearsay. Egypt, as he tells us himself, he knew at first hand as far as Elephantine, modern Assuan, and beyond that only by question and hearsay. His knowledge of Cyrene in North Africa has the flavor of first-hand knowledge, as also do his references to various places in south Italy and Sicily. In his writings are indications that he was thoroughly familiar with Athens, attracted no doubt like other writers and artists by the intellectual climate of the city which was then in its heyday.

Did Herodotus' histories grow out of his travels or were the travels made for the sake of his historical inquiries? We do not know. Nor have we any sure indication of how the traveller supported himself. His interest in means of transportation and in the exotic products of distant lands have been taken to imply activity in trade, and Herodotus, like many a modern Greek traveller, may well have done a little business on the side. He is reported to have given public readings of his work at Olympia and at Athens, but such recitals are not likely to have yielded a regular income.

The sketchy state of our knowledge of Herodotus' life is more than compensated by the completeness of his *Histories*. Despite a few minor inconsistencies and unfulfilled promises, there can be little doubt that the great work was essentially carried out as planned; this was in striking contrast to the unfinished lifework of Thucydides. And whereas we now have only a few scattered scraps of the work of earlier historians, Herodotus' nine books are intact, their text attested by a goodly number of mediaeval manuscripts. Not only are Herodotus' *Histories* the first well-preserved work of Greek historical writing, they are the oldest substantial surviving volume of Greek prose.

The theme of the *Histories* is set forth at the very beginning with the crisp precision of an inscription on a Greek statue base. The writer's purpose, he tells us, was twofold: to preserve from oblivion the great deeds of both the Greek and the Asiatic peoples and, especially, to record the reasons why they warred with one another. It was in fulfillment of the second of these purposes, to which he attached so much importance, that Herodotus looked into the early histories of the various peoples concerned. The Greek states come in for less consistent treatment than the eastern monarchies, as was perhaps natural for a Greek audience. But extended essays are devoted to the political history, the religion and the manners of the Lydians, Persians, Egyptians, Scythians, and Libyans. Similar treatment is promised in Book I for early Babylonia, though in fact no such part was written or, if written, it did not survive. The result is an uneven but richly colored panorama of the ancient world in one of the most interesting phases of its development. It was against this background that Herodotus then proceeded to describe in a more straightforward narrative the decisive clash between Greek and barbarian that was highlighted by the battles of Marathon, Thermopylae, Artemisium, Salamis, Plataea, and Mycale.

Cicero dubbed Herodotus "the father of history," and the title has never been seriously disputed. But back of the father were not a few other ancestors. Dionysius, the learned literary critic who shared Herodotus' birthplace, named a dozen such among many others whom he left unnamed. Evidently the ancient critics believed that Herodotus' work represented a fundamental advance in the development of this literary genre. We have too little of the writings of his predecessors to be able to say with assurance in what this advance consisted. There is reason to believe, however, that Herodotus worked on a much broader canvas than they, dealing not only with a single state but with relations among conflicting states, relying less on myth and hearsay, more on personal observation and inquiry, searching, above all, for the underlying causes that motivated peoples in their relations with one another.

The cause of our author's long continued popularity is easier to establish. His nine books contain a marvelously rich assortment of geography, ethnology, religion, biography, as well as political and military history, a combination that has won great popularity in more recent times for the writings of H. G. Wells. Style also had much to do with Herodotus' success. He is a marvelous storyteller with a sure feeling for what will hold an audience. The free use of speeches further increases the fresh, direct quality of the narrative. In all this and more Herodotus was following in the tradition of the Homeric epic, while at the same time, as Dionysius of Halicarnassus observed, he was the first writer to make prose as attractive as poetry. Finally, any sensitive reader must respond to the personality of the author that permeates the whole book: his zest for learning about the world, his warmth of feeling for his characters, his shrewd yet balanced judgments of men and peoples.

The illustrator of the present volume is surely a man after Herodotus' own heart. In his work, Joseph Farber has taken this approach to photography: "to use photography to tell about things that have interested me." He has travelled widely, in America and Europe, in Asia and Africa, always with zest and a keen eye for the interesting. The photographs included in this book are a selection from the many taken in the course of three years of travel in Greece and Egypt with Herodotus in mind. These splendid and carefully chosen illustrations will add a new dimension to the *Histories*, and they will surely enhance the pleasure of the reader whether he comes to the historian as a new or as an old friend. Had the camera existed in Herodotus' day he would certainly have exploited it to the full.

Homer A. Thompson
INSTITUTE FOR ADVANCED STUDY
PRINCETON

Bust of Herodotus, Roman copy, found in Egypt.

ANCIENT KINGS OF ASIA

IN this book, the result of my inquiries into history, I hope to do two things: to preserve the memory of the past by putting on record the astonishing achievements both of our own and of the Asiatic peoples; secondly, and more particularly, to show how the two races came into conflict.

Persian historians put the responsibility for the quarrel on the Phoenicians. These people came originally from the coasts of the Indian Ocean; and as soon as they had penetrated into the Mediterranean and settled in that part of the country where they are to-day, they took to making long trading voyages. Loaded with Egyptian and Assyrian goods, they called at various places along the coast, including Argos, in those days the most important of the countries now called by the general name of Hellas.

The traders often stole women and the Greeks did the same, among them, Medea, the daughter of the king of Colchis.*

The accounts go on to say that some forty or fifty years afterwards Paris, the son of Priam,

---

*NOTE TO THE READER: The text of Herodotus' Histories has been abridged in order to focus on the main events leading up to and through the wars between Persia and Greece. Commentary added to the Sélincourt translation is set in italic type.

was inspired by these stories to steal a wife for himself out of Greece, being confident that he would not have to pay for the venture any more than the Greeks had done. And that was how he came to carry off Helen.

The first idea of the Greeks after the rape was to send a demand for satisfaction and for Helen's return. The demand was met by a reference to the seizure of Medea and the injustice of expecting satisfaction from people to whom they themselves had refused it, not to mention the fact that they had kept the girl.

Thus far there had been nothing worse than woman-stealing on both sides. The Asiatics, according to the Persians, took the seizure of the women lightly enough, but not so the Greeks: the Greeks, merely on account of a girl from Sparta, raised a big army, invaded Asia and destroyed the empire of Priam. From that root sprang their belief in the perpetual enmity of the Grecian world towards them—Asia with its various foreign-speaking peoples belonging to the Persians, Europe and the Greek states being, in their opinion, quite separate and distinct from them.

Such then is the Persian story. In their view it was the capture of Troy that first made them enemies of the Greeks.

1

Menelaus and Helen

The sovereignty of Lydia, after belonging to the Heraclids for twenty-two generations—505 years—went to the Mermnadae: Gyges, then his son Alyattes, then his son Croesus. This is how Candaules, a Heraclid, lost the sovereignty.

Candaules conceived a passion for his own wife, and thought she was the most beautiful woman on earth. To this fancy of his there was an unexpected sequel.

In the king's bodyguard was a fellow he

2

particularly liked whose name was Gyges, son of Dascylus. With him Candaules not only discussed his most important business, but even used to make him listen to eulogies of his wife's beauty.

One day the king (who was doomed to a bad end) said to Gyges: 'It appears you don't believe me when I tell you how lovely my wife is. Well, a man always believes his eyes better than his ears; so do as I tell you—contrive to see her naked.'

Gyges gave a cry of horror. 'Master,' he said, 'what an improper suggestion! Do you tell me to look at the queen when she has no clothes on? No, no: "off with her skirt, off with her shame"—you know what they say of women. Let us learn from experience. Right and wrong were distinguished long ago—and I'll tell you one thing that is right: a man should mind his own business. I do not doubt that your wife is the most beautiful of women; so for goodness' sake do not ask me to behave like a criminal.'

Thus he did his utmost to decline the king's invitation, because he was afraid of what might happen if he accepted it.

The king, however, told him not to distress himself. 'There is nothing to be afraid of,' he said, 'either from me or my wife. I am not laying a trap for you; and as for her, I promise she will do you no harm. I'll manage so that she doesn't even know that you have seen her. Look: I will hide you behind the open door of our bedroom. My wife will follow me in to bed. Near the door there's a chair—she will put her clothes on it as she takes them off, one by one. You will be able to watch her with perfect ease. Then, while she's walking away from the chair towards the bed with her back to you, slip away through the door—and mind she doesn't catch you.'

Gyges, since he was unable to avoid it, consented, and when bedtime came Candaules brought him to the room. Presently the queen arrived, and Gyges watched her walk in and put her clothes on the chair. Then, just as she had turned her back and was going to bed, he slipped softly out of the room. Unluckily, the queen saw him.

At once she realized what her husband had done. But she did not betray the shame she felt by screaming, or even let it appear that she had noticed anything. Instead she silently resolved to have her revenge. For with the Lydians, as with most barbarian races, it is thought highly indecent even for a man to be seen naked.

For the moment she kept her mouth shut and did nothing; but at dawn the next morning she sent for Gyges after preparing the most trustworthy of her servants for what was to come. There was nothing unusual in his being asked to attend upon the queen; so Gyges answered the summons without any suspicion that she knew what had occurred on the previous night.

'Gyges,' she said, as soon as he presented himself, 'there are two courses open to you, and you may take your choice between them. Kill Candaules and seize the throne, with me as your wife; or die yourself on the spot, so that never again may your blind obedience to the king tempt you to see what you have no right to see. One of you must die: either my husband, the author of this wicked plot; or you, who have outraged propriety by seeing me naked.'

For a time Gyges was too much astonished to speak. At last he found words and begged the queen not to force him to make so difficult a choice. But it was no good; he soon saw that he really was faced with the alternatives, either of murdering his master, or of being murdered himself. He made his choice—to live.

'Tell me,' he said, 'since you drive me against my will to kill the king, how shall we set on him?'

'We will attack him when he is asleep,' was the answer; 'and on the very spot where he showed me to you naked.'

All was made ready for the attempt. The queen would not let Gyges go or give him any chance of escaping the dilemma: either Candaules or he must die. Night came, and he followed her into the bedroom. She put a knife into his hand, and hid him behind the same door as before. Then, when Candaules was asleep, he crept from behind the door and struck.

Thus Gyges usurped the throne and married the queen.

Later he had his power confirmed by an oracle from Delphi. The Lydians, indignant at the murder of Candaules, were prepared to

A Persian servant

fight; however, they managed to agree with the supporters of Gyges that he should continue to reign if the oracle declared that he was really the king; if on the other hand the oracle should declare against him, he should restore the throne to the Heraclids.

The answer of the oracle was in favour of Gyges, so his royal power was established. Nevertheless the Priestess of the Shrine added that the Heraclids would have their revenge on Gyges in the fifth generation: a prophecy to which neither the Lydians nor their kings paid any attention, until it was actually fulfilled.

Croesus, the Lydian, became very powerful and wealthy, having subdued most of Asia west of the Halys River. He may have been the first foreigner to force tribute from the Greeks and to make alliances with them. Solon, the Athenian lawmaker, visited Croesus at Sardis and was shown the riches of the kingdom. The King asked, "Who is the happiest of men you have ever seen?"—supposing himself to be the one. Solon first told about Tellus, a patriotic Athenian who had lived a happy life and had died a soldier. Croesus, sorely disappointed, then asked who the next happiest person was.

"Cleobis and Biton, two young men of Argos"

"Goddess Hera"

'Two young men of Argos,' was the reply; 'Cleobis and Biton. They had enough to live on comfortably; and their physical strength is proved not merely by their success in athletics, but much more by the following incident. The Argives were celebrating the festival of Hera, and it was most important that the mother of the two young men should drive to the temple in her ox-cart; but it so happened that the oxen were late in coming back from the fields. Her two sons therefore, as there was no time to lose, harnessed themselves to the cart and dragged it along, with their mother inside, for a distance of nearly six miles, until they reached the temple. After this exploit, which was witnessed by the assembled crowd, they had a most enviable death—a heaven-sent proof of how much better it is to be dead than alive. Men kept crowding round them and congratulating them on their strength, and women kept telling the mother how lucky she was to have such sons, when, in sheer pleasure at this public recognition of her sons' act, she prayed the goddess Hera, before whose shrine she stood, to grant Cleobis and Biton, who had brought her such honour, the greatest blessing that can fall to mortal man.

'After her prayer came the ceremonies of sacrifice and feasting; and the two lads, when all was over, fell asleep in the temple—and that

The Temple of Hera

was the end of them, for they never woke again.

'The Argives had statues made of them, which they sent to Delphi, as a mark of their particular respect.'

Croesus was vexed with Solon for giving the second prize for happiness to the two young Argives, and snapped out: 'That's all very well, my Athenian friend; but what of my own happiness? Is it so utterly contemptible that you won't even compare me with mere common folk like those you have mentioned?'

'Now if a man thus favoured dies as he has lived, he will be just the one you are looking for: the only sort of person who deserves to be called happy. But mark this: until he is dead, keep the word "happy" in reserve. Till then, he is not happy, but only lucky.'

There were struggles throughout Greece, battles between cities as well as fighting within them by individuals for power. Pisistratus, the dictator of Athens, had been exiled but through a hoax was allowed to return.

After the recovery of his power Pisistratus married Megacles' daughter, as he had agreed to do; but because of a story that Megacles' family, the Alcmaeonids, had a curse upon it, and because he already had grown-up sons of his own, he did not want children from his new wife, and to prevent her from having any refused normal intercourse and lay with her in an unnatural way. For a time his wife said nothing about this insult, but later—perhaps in answer to a question—she told her mother, and her mother told Megacles, who was so angry at the slight upon himself and his daughter, that he made up his quarrel with his political enemies. This new threat determined Pisistratus to get right out of the country. He went to Eretria and there discussed the situation with his sons. The view of Hippias that an attempt should be made to recover his lost position proved the most acceptable, and they began to collect contributions from the towns which were in any way favourable to their cause. Many towns gave large sums of money, but the contribution from Thebes was by far the most handsome. Time passed; they were joined by Argive mercenaries from the Peloponnese; a certain

Hippias as a young man

Lygdamis from Naxos freely offered his enthusiastic support, contributing both money and men; and at last—to cut the story short—everything was ready for the march on Athens. More than ten years had passed, when they left Eretria and returned.

Power in Asia shifted to the Scythians but they were driven out and Astyages became king.

Astyages had a daughter called Mandane, and he dreamed one night that she made water in such enormous quantities that it filled his city and swamped the whole of Asia. He told his dream to the Magi, whose business it was to interpret such things, and was much alarmed by what they said it meant. Consequently when Mandane was old enough to marry, he did not give her to some Mede of suitable rank, but was induced by his fear of the dream's significance to marry her to a Persian named Cambyses, a man he knew to be of good family and quiet habits—though he considered him much below a Mede even of middle rank.

Before Mandane and Cambyses had been married a year, Astyages had another dream. This time it was that a vine grew from his daughter's private parts and spread over Asia. As before, he told the interpreters about this dream, and then sent for his daughter, who was now pregnant. When she arrived, he kept her under strict watch, intending to make away with her child; for the fact was that the Magi had interpreted the dream to mean that his daughter's son would usurp his throne. To guard against this, Astyages, when Cyrus was born, sent for his kinsman Harpagus, the steward of his property, whom he trusted more than anyone, and said to him: 'I have some instructions for you, Harpagus, and mind you pay attention to them, whatever they may be. My safety depends upon you. If you neglect it and prefer to serve others, the day will come when you will be caught in your own trap. Get hold of Mandane's child—take it home and kill it. Then bury it how you please.'

The baby Cyrus was not killed but raised as the son of a herdsman. Early in life he showed qualities of leadership. His origins were discovered and Astyages planned revenge. He asked Harpagus for an explanation.

Harpagus' tale was a straightforward one, and Astyages, concealing his anger, first repeated to him the herdsman's account of the affair, and then, when he had gone over the whole story, ended by saying that all was well and the child was still alive; he had been greatly distressed, he added, by what had been done to it, and seriously concerned at the hatred he could not have failed to arouse in his daughter.

'And now,' he said, 'since things have taken this lucky turn, I want you to send your own son to visit the young newcomer; and come to dinner with me yourself, as I intend to celebrate my grandson's deliverance by a sacrifice to the gods to whom such rites belong.'

Harpagus bowed low when he heard what the king said, and went home much pleased with his invitation to dinner on so happy an occasion: it was a great thing, he thought, to

Achaemenid silver vase

have come off so lightly. As soon as he reached home, he sent his son—his only son, a boy of about thirteen years old—to Astyages' palace, with instructions to do whatever the king should command. Then in high glee he told his wife everything that had occurred.

When Harpagus' son arrived at the palace, Astyages had him butchered, cut up into joints and cooked, roasting some, boiling the rest, and having the whole properly prepared for the table. Dinnertime came and the guests assembled, with Harpagus amongst them. Dishes of mutton were placed in front of Astyages and of everybody else—except Harpagus. To Harpagus was served the flesh of his son: all of it, except the head, the hands, and the feet, which had been put separately on a platter covered with a lid.

When Harpagus thought he had eaten as much as he wanted, Astyages asked him if he had enjoyed his dinner. He answered that he had enjoyed it very much indeed, whereupon those whose business it was to do so brought in the boy's head, hands, and feet in the covered dish, stood by Harpagus' chair and told him to lift the lid and take what he fancied. Harpagus removed the cover and saw the fragments of his son's body. As he kept control of himself and did not lose his head at the dreadful sight, Astyages asked him if he knew what animal it was whose flesh he had eaten. 'I know, my lord,' was Harpagus' reply: 'and for my part—may the king's will be done.' He said no other word, but took up what remained of the flesh and went home, intending, I suppose, to bury all of it together. And that was how Harpagus was punished.

As predicted, Cyrus seized the throne from his father, with the help of Harpagus. Relations continued strained between Cyrus and the Ionians. After his death he was succeeded by his son Cambyses.

TRAVELS
IN EGYPT

CAMBYSES *planned an expedition against the Egyptians. The priests of Hephaestus at Memphis told Herodotus much about the Egyptians.*

I actually went to Thebes and Heliopolis for the express purpose of finding out if the priests in those cities would agree in what they told me with the priests at Memphis. It is at Heliopolis that the most learned of the Egyptian antiquaries are said to be found. I am not anxious to repeat what I was told about the Egyptian religion, apart from the mere names of their deities, for I do not think that any one nation knows much more about such things than any other; whatever I shall mention on the subject will be due simply to the exigencies of my story. As to practical matters, they all agreed in saying that the Egyptians by their study of astronomy discovered the solar year and were the first to divide it into twelve parts—and in my opinion their method of calculation is better than the Greek; for the Greeks, to make the seasons work out properly, intercalate a whole month every other year, while the Egyptians make the year consist of twelve months of thirty days each and every year intercalate five additional days, and so complete the regular circle of the seasons. They also told me that the

Egyptians first brought into use the names of the twelve gods, which the Greeks took over from them, and were the first to assign altars and images and temples to the gods, and to carve figures in stone. They proved the truth of most of these assertions, and went on to tell me that the first man to rule Egypt was Min, in whose time the whole country, except the district around Thebes, was marsh, none of the land below Lake Moeris—seven days' voyage up river from the sea—then showing above the water. I have little doubt that they were right in this; for it is clear to any intelligent observer, even if he has no previous information on the subject, that the Egypt to which we sail nowadays is, as it were, the gift of the river and has come only recently into the possession of its inhabitants. The same is true of the country above the lake for the distance of a three days' voyage: the priests said nothing to me about it, but it is, in fact, precisely the same type of country.

The following is a general description of the physical features of Egypt. If you take a cast of the lead a day's sail off-shore, you will get eleven fathoms, muddy bottom—which shows how far out the silt from the river extends. The country (*near the coast*) is broad and flat, with much swamp and mud.

Temple of Ptah (Hephaestus)

Farming in the shadow of the Pyramids

Pyramids of Mycerinus, Chephren and Cheops

A quarry for pyramid stone

Southward of Heliopolis the country narrows. It is confined on the one side by the range of the Arabian mountains which run north and south and then continue without a break in the direction of the Arabian Gulf. In these mountains are the quarries where the stone was cut for the pyramids at Memphis. This is the point where the range changes its direction and bends away towards the Arabian Gulf. I learnt that its greatest length from east to west is a two months' journey, and that towards its eastern limit frankincense is produced. On the Libyan side of Egypt there is another range of hills where the pyramids stand; these hills are rocky and covered with sand, and run in a southerly direction like the Arabian range before it bends eastward. Above Heliopolis, then, for a distance of four days' voyage up the river Egypt is narrow, and the extent of territory, for so important a country, is meagre enough. Between the two mountain ranges—the Libyan and Arabian—it is a level plain, in its narrowest part, so far as I could judge, not more than about two hundred furlongs across. South of this the country broadens again.

My own observation bears out the statement made to me by the priests that the greater part of the country I have described has been built up by silt from the Nile.

About why the Nile behaves precisely as it does I could get no information from the priests or anyone else. What I particularly wished to know was why the water begins to rise at the summer solstice, continues to do so for a hundred days, and then falls again at the end of that period, so that it remains low throughout the winter until the summer solstice comes round again in the following year. Nobody in Egypt could give me any explanation of this, in spite of my constant attempts to find out what was the peculiar property which made the Nile behave in the opposite way to other rivers, and why—another point on which I hoped for information—it was the only river to cause no breezes.

One theory of the flooding of the Nile is that the floods come from melting snow.

(*But*) kites and swallows remain throughout

Kites along the Nile

the year, and cranes migrate thither in winter to escape the cold weather of Scythia. But if there were any snow, however little, in the region through which the Nile flows and in which it rises, none of these things could possibly be; for they are contrary to reason.

Concerning the sources of the Nile, nobody I have spoken with, Egyptian, Libyan, or Greek, professed to have any knowledge, except the scribe who kept the register of the treasures of Athene in the Egyptian city of Sais. But even this person's account, though he pretended to exact knowledge, seemed to me hardly serious. He told me that between Syene, near Thebes, and Elephantine there were two mountains of conical shape called Crophi and Mophi; and that the springs of the Nile, which were of fathomless depth, flowed out from between them. Half of the water flowed northwards towards Egypt and half southwards towards Ethiopia. The fact that the springs were bottomless he said had been proved by the Egyp-

Elephantine Island

Defense wall at Syene

tian king Psammetichus, who had a rope made many thousands of fathoms long which he let down into the water without finding the bottom. I think myself that if there is any truth in this story of the scribe's, it indicates the presence of powerful whirlpools and eddies in the water, caused by its impact upon the mountains, and it was these eddies which prevented the sounding-line from reaching the bottom.

On this subject I could get no further information from anybody. I went as far as Elephantine to see what I could with my own eyes, but for the country still further south I had to be content with what I was told in answer to my questions.

The Egyptians had guardposts in various parts of the country: one at Elephantine against the Ethiopians, another in Daphnae at Pelusium against the Arabians and Assyrians, and

a third at Marea to keep a watch on Libya. The Persians have similar garrisons to-day both at Elephantine and Daphnae.

About Egypt I shall have a great deal more to relate because of the number of remarkable things which the country contains, and because of the fact that more monuments which beggar description are to be found there than anywhere else in the world. That is reason enough for my dwelling on it at greater length. Not only is the Egyptian climate peculiar to that country, and the Nile different in its behaviour from other rivers elsewhere, but the Egyptians themselves in their manners and customs seem to have reversed the ordinary practices of mankind. For instance, women attend market and are employed in trade, while men stay at home and do the weaving. In weaving the normal way is to work the threads of the weft upwards,

17

The Nile valley above Memphis

A shaved priest

but the Egyptians work them downwards. Men in Egypt carry loads on their heads, women on their shoulders; women pass water standing up, men sitting down. To ease themselves they go indoors, but eat outside in the streets, on the theory that what is unseemly but necessary should be done in private, and what is not unseemly should be done openly. No woman holds priestly office, either in the service of goddess or god; only men are priests in both cases. Sons are under no compulsion to support their parents if they do not wish to do so, but daughters must, whether they wish it or not. Elsewhere priests grow their hair long; in Egypt they shave their heads. In other nations the relatives of the deceased in time of mourning cut their hair, but the Egyptians, who shave at all other times, mark a death by letting the hair grow both on head and chin. They live with their animals—unlike the rest of the world, who live apart from them. Other men live on wheat and barley, but any Egyptian who does so is blamed for it, their bread being made from spelt, or *Zea* as some call it. Dough they knead with their feet, but clay with their hands—and even handle dung. They practise circumcision, while men of other nations—except those who have learnt from Egypt—leave their private parts as nature made them. Men in Egypt have two garments each, women only one. The ordinary practice at sea is to make sheets fast to ring-bolts fitted outboard; the Egyptians fit them inboard. In writing or calculating, instead of going, like the Greeks, from left to right, the Egyptians go from right to left—and obstinately maintain that theirs is the dexterous method, ours being left-handed and awkward. They have two sorts of writing, the sacred and the common. They are religious to excess, beyond any other nation in the world, and here are some of the customs which illustrate the fact: they drink from brazen cups which they scour every day—everyone, without exception. They wear linen clothes which they make a special point of continually washing. They circumcise themselves for cleanliness' sake, preferring to be clean rather than comely. The priests shave their bodies all over every other day to guard against the presence of lice, or anything else equally unpleasant, while they are about their religious duties; the priests, too, wear linen only, and shoes made from the papyrus plant—these materials, for dress and shoes, being the only ones allowed them. They bathe in cold water twice a day and twice every night—and observe innumerable other ceremonies besides. Their life, however, is not by any means all hardship, for they enjoy advantages too: for instance, they are free from all personal ex-

pense, having bread made for them out of the sacred grain, and a plentiful daily supply of goose-meat and beef, with wine in addition. Fish they are forbidden to touch; and as for beans, they cannot even bear to look at them, because they imagine they are unclean (in point of fact the Egyptians never sow beans, and even if any happen to grow wild, they will not eat them, either raw or boiled). They do not have a single priest for each god, but a number, of which one is chief-priest, and when a chief-

Circumcision

The Ramesseum

priest dies his son is appointed to succeed him. Bulls are considered the property of the god Epaphus—or Apis—and are therefore tested in the following way: a priest appointed for the purpose examines the animal, and if he finds even a single black hair upon him, pronounces him unclean; he goes over him with the greatest care, first making him stand up, then lie on his back, after which he pulls out his tongue to see if that, too, is 'clean' according to the recognized marks—what those are I will explain later. He also inspects the tail to make sure the hair on it grows properly; then, if the animal passes all these tests successfully, the priest marks him by twisting round his horns a band of papyrus which he seals with wax and stamps with his signet ring. The bull is finally taken away, and the penalty is death for anybody who sacrifices an animal which has not been marked in this manner. The method of sacrifice is as follows: they take the beast (one of those marked with the seal) to the appropriate altar and light a fire; then, after pouring a libation of wine and invoking the god by name, they slaughter it, cut off its head, and flay the carcase. The head is loaded with curses and taken away—if there happen to be Greek traders in the market, it is sold to them; if not, it is thrown into the river. The curses they pronounce take the form of a prayer that any disaster which threatens either themselves or their country may be diverted and fall upon the severed head

23

Columns and shadows (top), The Temple of Luxor (bottom)

*Sesostris
(Ramses II)*

Colossi of Memnon, guardians of the Pharaohs' tombs

The Temple of Amun, hypostyle hall

Nefertari, wife of Sesostris (Ramses II)

of the beast. Both the libation and the practice of cutting off the heads of sacrificial beasts are common to all Egyptians in all their sacrifices, and the latter explains why it is that no Egyptian will use the head of any sort of animal for food. The methods of disembowelling and burning are various, and I will describe the one which is followed in the worship of the goddess whom they consider the greatest and honour with the most important festival. In this case,

when they have flayed the bull, they first pray and then take its paunch out whole, leaving the intestines and fat inside the body; next they cut off the legs, shoulders, neck, and rump, and stuff the carcase with loaves of bread, honey, raisins, figs, frankincense, myrrh, and other aromatic substances; finally they pour a quantity of oil over the carcase and burn it. They always fast before a sacrifice, and while the fire is consuming it they beat their breasts. That

27

Avenue of Rams

part of the ceremony done, they serve a meal out of the portions left over.

All Egyptians use bulls and bull-calves for sacrifice, if they have passed the test for 'cleanness'; but they are forbidden to sacrifice cows, on the ground that they are sacred to Isis. The statues of Isis show a female figure with cow's horns, like the Greek representations of Io, and of all animals cows are universally held by the Egyptians in the greatest reverence. This is the reason why no Egyptian, man or woman, will kiss a Greek, or use a Greek knife, spit, or cauldron, or even eat the flesh of a bull known to be clean, if it has been cut with a Greek knife.

The Egyptians meet in solemn assembly not once a year only, but on a number of occasions, the most important and best attended being the festival of Artemis at Bubastis: second in importance is the assembly at Busiris—a city in the middle of the Delta, containing a vast temple dedicated to Isis, the Egyptian equivalent of Demeter, in whose honour the meeting is held. Then there are the assemblies in honour of Athene at Sais, of the Sun at Heliopolis, of Leto at Buto, and of Ares at Papremis. The pro-

cedure at Bubastis is this: they come in barges, men and women together, a great number in each boat; on the way, some of the women keep up a continual clatter with castanets and some of the men play flutes, while the rest, both men and women, sing and clap their hands. Whenever they pass a town on the river-bank, they bring the barge close in-shore, some of the women continuing to act as I have said, while others shout abuse at the women of the place, or start dancing, or stand up and hitch up their skirts. When they reach Bubastis they celebrate the festival with elaborate sacrifices, and more wine is consumed than during all the rest of the year. The numbers that meet there, are, according to native report, as many as seven hundred thousand men and women—excluding children.

It was the Egyptians who first made it an offence against piety to have intercourse with women in temples, or to enter temples after intercourse without having previously washed. Hardly any nation except the Egyptians and Greeks has any such scruple, but nearly all consider men and women to be, in this respect, no different from animals, which, whether they

◀ *Temple of Amun, Karnak*

Bubastis

are beasts or birds, they constantly see coupling in temples and sacred places—and if the god concerned had any objection to this, he would not allow it to occur. Such is the theory, but, in spite of it, I must continue to disapprove the practice. The Egyptians are meticulous in their observance of this point, as indeed they are in everything else which concerns their religion.

There are not a great many wild animals in Egypt, in spite of the fact that it borders on Libya. Such as there are—both wild and tame— are without exception held to be sacred.

Anyone who deliberately kills one of these animals, is punished with death; should one be

killed accidentally, the penalty is whatever the priests choose to impose; but for killing an ibis or a hawk, whether deliberately or not, the penalty is inevitably death.

The number, already large, of domestic animals would have been greatly increased, were it not for an odd thing that happens to the cats. The females, when they have kittens, avoid the toms, greatly to the distress of the latter who are thus deprived of their satisfaction. The toms, however, get over the difficulty very ingeniously, for they either openly seize, or secretly steal, the kittens and kill them—but without eating them—and the result is that the females, deprived of their kittens and wanting more (for their maternal instinct is very strong), go off to look for mates again. What happens when a house catches fire is most extraordinary: nobody takes the least trouble to put it out, for it is only the cats that matter; everyone stands in a row, a little distance from his neighbour, trying to protect the cats, who nevertheless slip through the line, or jump over it, and hurl themselves into the flames. This causes the Egyptians deep distress. All the inmates of a house where a cat has died a natural death shave their eyebrows, and when a dog dies they shave the whole body including the head. Cats which have died are taken to Bubastis, where they are embalmed and buried in sacred receptacles; dogs are buried, also in sacred burial-places, in the towns where they belong. Weasels are buried in the same way as dogs; field-mice and hawks are taken to Buto, ibises to Hermopolis. Bears, which are scarce, and wolves (which in Egypt are not much bigger than foxes) are buried wherever they happen to be found lying dead.

The crocodile during the four winter months takes no food. It is a four-footed, amphibious creature, lays and hatches its eggs on land, where it spends the greater part of the day, and stays all night in the river, where the water is warmer than the night-air and the dew. The difference in size between the young and the full-grown crocodile is greater than in any other known creature; for a crocodile's egg is hardly bigger than a goose's, and the young when hatched is small in proportion, yet it grows to a size of some twenty-three feet long or even more. It has eyes like a pig's and great fang-like teeth, and is the only animal to have no tongue and a stationary lower jaw; for when it eats it brings the upper jaw down upon the under. It has powerful claws and a scaly hide, which on its back is impenetrable. It cannot see under water, though on land its sight is remarkably quick. One result of its spending so much time in the water is that the inside of its mouth gets covered with leeches. Other animals avoid the crocodile, as do all birds too with one exception—the sandpiper, or Egyptian plover: this bird is of service to the crocodile and lives, in consequence, in the greatest amity with him; for when the crocodile comes ashore and lies with his mouth wide open (which he generally does facing towards the west), the bird hops in and swallows the leeches. The crocodile enjoys this, and never, in consequence, hurts the bird. Some Egyptians reverence the crocodile as a sacred beast; others do not, but treat it as an enemy. The strongest belief in its sanctity is to be found in Thebes and round about Lake Moeris; in these places they keep one particular crocodile, which they tame, putting rings made of glass or gold into its ears and bracelets round its front feet, and giving it special food and ceremonial offerings. In fact, while these creatures are alive they treat them with every kindness, and, when they die, embalm them and bury them in sacred tombs. On the other hand, in the neighbourhood of Elephantine crocodiles are not considered sacred animals at all, but are eaten.

The hippopotamus is held sacred in the district of Papremis, but not elsewhere. This animal has four legs, cloven hoofs like an ox, a snub nose, a horse's mane and tail, conspicuous

Osiris, unfinished

Ceremonial dance

A sacred crocodile

tusks, a voice like a horse's neigh, and is about the size of a very large ox. Its hide is so thick and tough that when dried it can be made into spear-shafts.

The Egyptians who live in the cultivated parts of the country, by their practice of keeping records of the past, have made themselves much the best historians of any nation of which I have had experience. I will describe some of their habits: every month for three successive days they purge themselves, for their health's sake, with emetics and clysters, in the belief that all diseases come from the food a man eats; and it is a fact—even apart from this precaution—that next to the Libyans they are the healthiest people in the world. I should put this down myself to the absence of changes in the climate; for change, and especially change of weather, is the prime cause of disease. They eat loaves made from spelt—*cyllestes* is their word for them—and drink a wine made from barley, as they have no vines in the country. Some kinds of fish they eat raw, either dried in the sun, or salted; quails, too, they eat raw, and ducks and various small birds, after pickling them in brine; other sorts of birds and fish, apart from those which are considered sacred, they either roast or boil. When the rich give a party and the meal is finished, a man carries round amongst the guests a wooden image of a corpse in a coffin, carved and painted to look as much like the real thing as possible, and anything from eighteen inches to three feet long; he shows it to each guest in turn, and says: 'Look upon this body as you drink and enjoy yourself; for you will be just like it when you are dead.'

The practice of medicine they split up into separate parts, each doctor being responsible for the treatment of only one disease. There are, in consequence, innumerable doctors, some specializing in diseases of the eyes, others of the head, others of the teeth, others of the stomach and so on; while others, again, deal with the sort of troubles which cannot be exactly localized. As regards mourning and funerals, when a distinguished man dies all the women of the household plaster their heads

Egyptian cat

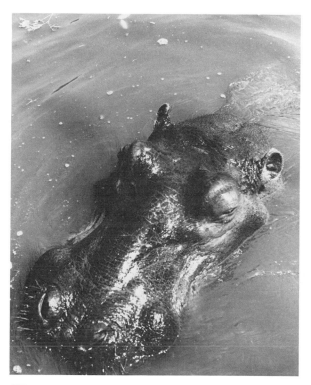

Hippopotamus

and faces with mud, then, leaving the body indoors, perambulate the town with the dead man's female relatives, their dresses fastened with a girdle, and beat their bared breasts. The men too, for their part, follow the same procedure, wearing a girdle and beating themselves like the women. The ceremony over, they take the body to be embalmed.

Embalming is a distinct profession. The embalmers, when a body is brought to them, produce specimen models in wood, painted to resemble nature, and graded in quality; the best and most expensive kind is said to represent a being whose name I shrink from mentioning in this connection; the next best is somewhat inferior and cheaper, while the third sort is cheapest of all. After pointing out these differences in quality, they ask which of the three is required, and the kinsmen of the dead man, having agreed upon a price, go away and leave the embalmers to their work. The most perfect process is as follows: as much as possible of the brain is extracted through the nostrils with an iron hook, and what the hook cannot reach is rinsed out with drugs; next the flank is laid open with a flint knife and the whole contents of the abdomen removed; the cavity is then thoroughly cleansed and washed out, first with palm wine and again with an infusion of pounded spices. After that it is filled with pure bruised myrrh, cassia, and every other aromatic substance with the exception of frankincense, and sewn up again, after which the body is placed in natrum, covered entirely over, for seventy days—never longer. When this period, which must not be exceeded, is over, the body is washed and then wrapped from head to foot in linen cut into strips and smeared on the under side with gum, which is commonly used by the Egyptians instead of glue. In this condition the body is given back to the family, who have a wooden case made, shaped like the human figure, into which it is put. The case is then sealed up and stored in a sepulchral chamber, upright against the wall.

Up to this point I have described the life of the Egyptians who live south of the marsh-country; those who inhabit the marshes are in most things much the same as the rest; and they also practise monogamy, as the Greeks do; nevertheless they are peculiar in certain ways which they have discovered of living more cheaply: for instance, they gather the water-lilies (called lotus by the Egyptians), which grow in great abundance when the river is full and floods the neighbouring flats, and dry them in the sun; then from the centre of each blossom they pick out something which resembles a poppyhead, grind it, and make it into loaves which they bake. The root of this plant is also edible; it is round, about as big as an apple, and tastes sweet. There is another

An Egyptian physician

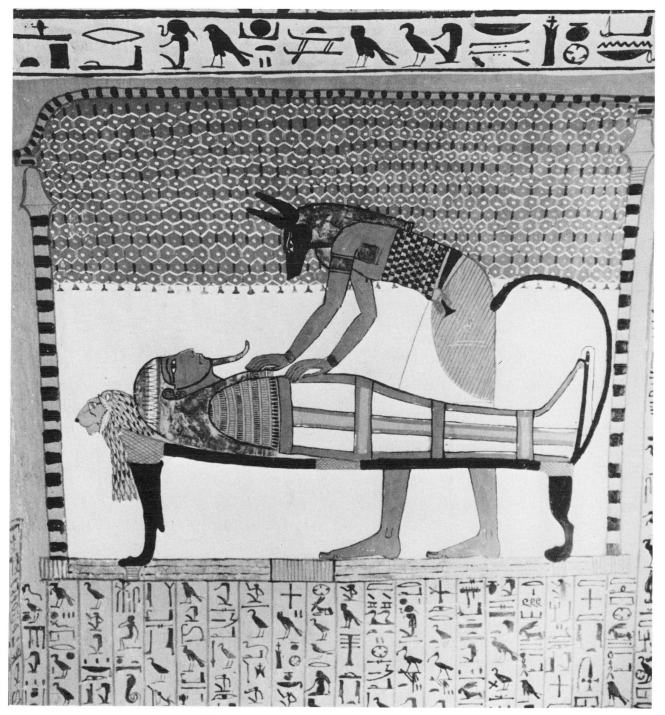

"Embalming is a distinct profession"

Lotus blossoms

Papyrus

kind of lily to be found in the river; this resembles a rose, and its fruit is formed on a separate stalk from that which bears the blossom, and has very much the looks of a wasp's comb. The fruit contains a number of seeds, about the size of an olive-stone, which are good to eat either green or dried. They pull up the annual crop of papyrus-reed which grows in the marshes, cut the stalks in two, and eat the lower part, about eighteen inches in length, first baking it in a closed pan, heated red-hot, if they want to enjoy it to perfection. The upper section of the stalk is used for some other purpose. Some of these people, however, live upon nothing but fish, which they gut as soon as they catch them, and eat after drying them in the sun.

The Nile boats used for carrying freight are built of acantha wood—the acantha in form resembles the lotus of Cyrene, and exudes gum. They cut short planks, about three feet long, from this tree, and the method of construction is to lay them together like bricks and through-fasten them with long spikes set close together, and then, when the hull is complete, to lay the deck-beams across on top. The boats have no ribs and are caulked from inside with papyrus. They are given a single steering-oar, which is driven down through the keel; the masts are of acantha wood, the sails of papyrus. These vessels cannot sail up the river without a good leading wind, but have to be towed from the banks; and for dropping downstream with the

Ancient Nile boat

current they are handled as follows: each vessel is equipped with a raft made of tamarisk wood, with a rush mat fastened on top of it, and a stone with a hole through it weighing some four hundredweight; the raft and the stone are made fast to the vessel with ropes, fore and aft respectively, so that the raft is carried rapidly forward by the current and pulls the 'bars' (as these boats are called) after it, while the stone, dragging along the bottom astern, acts as a check and gives her steerage-way. There are a great many of these vessels on the Nile, some of them of enormous carrying capacity.

The priests told me that it was Min, the first king of Egypt, who raised the dam which protects Memphis from the floods. The river used to flow along the base of the sandy hills on the Libyan border, and this monarch, by damming it up at the bend about a hundred furlongs south of Memphis, drained the original channel and diverted it to a new one half-way between the two lines of hills. To this day the elbow which the Nile forms here, where it is forced into its new channel, is most carefully watched by the Persians, who strengthen the dam every year; for should the river burst it, Memphis might be completely overwhelmed. On the land which had been drained by the diversion of the river, King Min built the city which is now called Memphis—it lies in the narrow part of Egypt—and afterwards on the north and west sides of the town excavated a lake, communicating with the river, which itself protects it on the east. In addition to this the priests told me that he built there the large and very remarkable temple of Hephaestus.

As none of the other kings on the priests' roll left any memorial at all, I will pass on to say something of Sesostris, who succeeded them.* Sesostris, the priests said, sailed first with a fleet of warships from the Arabian gulf along the coast of the Indian Ocean, subduing the coastal tribes as he went, until he found that shoal water made further progress impossible; then on his return to Egypt (still according to the priests' account) he raised a powerful army

* Sesostris is assumed to be Ramses II.

and marched across the continent, reducing to subjection every nation in his path. Whenever he encountered a courageous enemy who fought valiantly for freedom, he erected pillars on the spot inscribed with his own name and country, and a sentence to indicate that by the might of his armed forces he had won the victory; if, however, a town fell easily into his hands without a struggle, he made an addition to the inscription on the pillar—for not only did he record upon it the same facts as before, but added a picture of a woman's genitals, meaning to show that the people of that town were no braver than women. Thus his victorious progress through Asia continued, until he entered Europe and defeated the Scythians and Thracians; this, I think, was the furthest point the Egyptian army reached, for the memorial columns are to be seen in this part of the country but not beyond.

Sesostris was the only Egyptian king to rule Ethiopia. As memorials of his reign he left stone statues of himself and his wife, each forty-five feet high, and statues thirty feet high of each of his four sons. They were erected in front of the temple of Hephaestus. Long afterwards the priest of Hephaestus would not allow Darius the king of Persia to erect a statue of himself in front of these, because (as he put it) his deeds had not been as great as the deeds of Sesostris the Egyptian; the conquests of Seostris, no less extensive than those of Darius, included the Scythians, whom Darius had been unable to subdue; it was not right, therefore, that he should put his statue in front of those dedicated by a monarch, whose achievements he had failed to surpass. Darius, they say, admitted the truth of this.

Up to the time of Rhampsinitus, Egypt was excellently governed and very prosperous; but his successor Cheops (to continue the account which the priests gave me) brought the country into all sorts of misery. He closed all the temples, then, not content with excluding his subjects from the practice of their religion, compelled them without exception to labour as slaves for his own advantage. Some were forced to drag blocks of stone from the quarries in

A valley of tombs

the Arabian hills to the Nile, where they were ferried across and taken over by others, who hauled them to the Libyan hills. The work went on in three-monthly shifts, a hundred thousand men in a shift. It took ten years of this oppressive slave-labour to build the track along which the blocks were hauled—a work, in my opinion, of hardly less magnitude than the pyramid itself, for it is five furlongs in length, sixty feet wide, forty-eight feet high at its highest point, and constructed of polished stone blocks decorated with carvings of animals. To build it took, as I said, ten years—including the underground sepulchral chambers on the hill where the pyramids stand; a cut was made from the Nile, so that the water from it turned the site of these into an island. To build the pyramid itself took twenty years; it is square at the base, its height (800 feet) equal to the length of each side; it is of polished stone blocks beautifully fitted, none of the blocks being less than thirty feet long. The method employed was to build it in tiers, or steps, if you prefer the word—something like battlements running up the slope of a hill; when the base was complete, the blocks for the first tier above it were lifted from ground level by cranes or sheerlegs, made of short timbers; on this first tier there was another lifting-crane which raised the blocks a stage higher, then yet another which raised them higher still. Each tier, or storey, had its crane—or it may be that they used the same one, which, being easy to carry, they shifted up from stage to stage as soon as its load was dropped into place. Both methods are mentioned, so I give them both here. The finishing-off of the pyramid was begun at the top and continued downwards, ending with the lowest parts nearest the ground. An inscription is cut upon it in Egyptian char-

acters recording the amount spent on radishes, onions, and leeks for the labourers, and I remember distinctly that the interpreter who read me the inscription said the sum was 1600 talents of silver. If this is true, how much must have been spent in addition on bread and clothing for the labourers during all those years the building was going on—not to mention the time it took (not a little, I should think) to quarry and haul the stone, and to construct the underground chamber?

But no crime was too great for Cheops: when he was short of money, he sent his daughter to a bawdy-house with instructions to charge a certain sum—they did not tell me how much. This she actually did, adding to it a further transaction of her own; for with the intention of leaving something to be remembered by

Sphinx

The Step Pyramid

after her death, she asked each of her customers to give her a block of stone, and of these stones (the story goes) was built the middle pyramid of the three which stand in front of the great pyramid. It is a hundred and fifty feet square.

Cheops reigned for fifty years, according to the Egyptians' account, and was succeeded after his death by his brother Chephren. Chephren was not better than his predecessor; his rule was equally oppressive, and, like Cheops, he built a pyramid, but of a smaller size (I measured both of them myself). It has no underground chambers, and no channel was dug, as in the case of Cheops' pyramid, to bring to it the water from the Nile. The cutting of the canal, as I have already said, makes the site of the pyramid of Cheops into an island, and there his body is supposed to be. The pyramid of Chephren lies close to the great pyramid of Cheops; it is forty feet lower than the latter, but otherwise of the same dimensions; its lower course is of the coloured stone of Ethiopia. Both these pyramids stand on the same hill,

41

Cheops' daughter's pyramid

which is about a hundred feet in height. Chephren reigned for fifty-six years—so the Egyptians reckon a period of a hundred and six years, all told, during which the temples were never opened for worship and the country was reduced in every way to the greatest misery. The Egyptians can hardly bring themselves to mention the names of Cheops and Chephren, so great is their hatred of them; they even call the pyramids after Philitis, a shepherd who at that time fed his flocks in the neighborhood.

The next king of Egypt after Chephren was Mycerinus, the son of Cheops. Mycerinus, reversing his father's policy of which he did not approve, reopened the temples and allowed his subjects, who had been brought into such abject slavery, to resume the practice of their religion and their normal work. Of all kings who ruled in Egypt he had the greatest reputation for justice in the decision of legal causes, and for this the Egyptians give him higher praise than any other monarch; for apart from the general equity of his judgements, he used to compensate out of his own property any man who was dissatisfied with the result of his suit, and so leave him nothing to complain of.

During the reign of Anysis, the blind king, Egypt was invaded by Ethiopia and ruled by Sebacos.

Nevertheless, before, Egypt was, indeed, ruled by gods, who lived on earth amongst men, sometimes one of them, sometimes another being supreme above the rest. The last of them was Orus the son of Osiris—Orus is the Apollo, Osiris the Dionysus, of the Greeks. It was Orus who vanquished Typhon and was the last god to sit upon the throne of Egypt.

So far the Egyptians themselves have been my authority; but in what follows I shall relate what other people, too, are willing to accept in the history of this country, with a few points

Amasis' temple

Sebacos

added from my own observation. After the reign of Sethos, the priest of Hephaestus, the Egyptians for a time were freed from monarchical government. Unable, however, to do without a king for long, they divided Egypt into twelve regions and appointed a king for each of them. United by intermarriage, the twelve kings governed in mutual friendliness on the understanding that none of them should attempt to oust any of the others, or to increase his power at the expense of the rest. They came to the understanding, and ensured that the terms of it should be rigorously kept, because, at the time when the twelve kingdoms were first established, an oracle had declared that the one who should pour a libation from a bronze cup in the temple of Hephaestus would become master of all Egypt.

43

Pyramid near the labyrinth

To strengthen the bond between them, they decided to leave a common memorial of their reigns, and for this purpose constructed a labyrinth a little above Lake Moeris, near the place called the City of Crocodiles. I have seen this building, and it is beyond my power to describe; it must have cost more in labour and money than all the walls and public works of the Greeks put together—though no one would deny that the temples at Ephesus and Samos are remarkable buildings. The pyramids, too, are astonishing structures, each one of them equal to many of the most ambitious works of Greece; but the labyrinth surpasses them. It has twelve covered courts—six in a row facing north, six south—the gates of the one range

exactly fronting the gates of the other, with a continuous wall round the outside of the whole.

After his accession to the throne, Psammis was visited by a deputation from Elis. These men had come to boast of the excellence of the organization of the Olympic Games, which, they thought, could not possibly be run better or more fairly, even by the Egyptians themselves, who were the ablest people in the world. When the Eleans had explained the reason for their visit, the king summoned a meeting of the most learned of his subjects, who proceeded to ask questions of the Eleans, and received in reply a full account of their method of organizing the Games. Having described in detail everything they did, the Eleans then said that

*The Olympic
playing field*

*The way to
Olympia*

they had come to find out if the Egyptians could think of anything fairer to suggest. The Egyptians, after considering the matter, asked if the Eleans allowed any people from their own city to compete in the Games, and when they were informed that competition was free and open to members of all the Greek states, including Elis, they expressed the opinion that to organize the games on such a principle was not fair at all; for it was quite impossible, when men from one's own city took part in some event, not to favour them at the expense of the strangers. If they really wanted fair play at the Games, and if that was indeed the purpose of their visit to Egypt, then (they said) they should open the various events to visitors only, and not allow anyone from Elis to compete.

The king Apries ruled for twenty-five years, but when his expedition against Cyrene failed, the Egyptians rose up and overthrew him.

When Apries had been deposed, Amasis came to the throne. He belonged to the district of Sais and was a native of the town called Siuph. At first the Egyptians were inclined to be contemptuous, and did not think much of him because of his humble and undistinguished origin; but later on he cleverly brought them to heel, without having recourse to harsh measures. Amongst his innumerable treasures, he had a gold foot-bath, which he and his guests used on occasion to wash their feet in. This he broke up, and with the material had a statue made to one of the gods, which he then set up in what he thought the most suitable spot in the city. The Egyptians constantly coming upon the statue, treated it with profound reverence, and as soon as Amasis heard of the effect it had upon them, he called a meeting and revealed the fact that the deeply revered statue was once a foot-bath, which they washed their feet and pissed and vomited in. He went on to say that his own case was much the same, in that once he had been only an ordinary person and was now their king; so that just as they had come to revere the transformed foot-bath, so they had better pay honour and respect to him too. In this way the Egyptians were persuaded to accept him as their master.

DARIUS
BECOMES
KING

AMASIS was on the throne when Cyrus' son Cambyses prepared his invasion of Egypt at the head of an army drawn from various subject nations and including both Ionian and Aeolian Greeks.

While ruling Egypt, Cambyses made several unsuccessful attempts to conquer neighboring countries. He never understood Egyptian customs and was hated by the people; they considered him mad.

Apis—or Epaphus—is the calf of a cow which is never afterwards able to have another. The Egyptian belief is that a flash of light descends upon the cow from heaven, and this causes her to conceive Apis. The Apis-calf has distinctive marks: it is black, with a white diamond on its forehead, the image of an eagle on its back, the hairs on its tail double, and a scarab under its tongue. The priests brought the animal and Cambyses, half mad as he was, drew his dagger, aimed a blow at its belly, but missed and struck its thigh. Then he laughed, and said to the priests: 'Do you call that a god, you poor blockheads? Are your gods flesh and blood? Do they feel the prick of steel? No doubt a god like that is good enough for the Egyptians; but you won't get away with trying to make a fool of me.' He then ordered the priests to be whipped by the men whose business it was to carry out such punishments, and any Egyptian who was found still keeping holiday to be put to death. In this way the festival was broken up, the priests punished, and Apis, who lay in the temple for a time wasting away from the wound in his thigh, finally died and was buried by the priests without the knowledge of Cambyses.

Cambyses had his brother Smerdis killed, fearing Smerdis would usurp his power. While Cambyses was with his army in Syria, two men of the caste of the Magus—one of them named Smerdis—secretly took over the throne, keeping the knowledge from the people. When Cambyses heard that Smerdis was on the throne, and thinking it was his brother, after all, he accidentally wounded himself in the thigh, the place where he had mortally wounded the sacred Apis-calf. He gathered leading Persians around him.

'I murdered my brother for nothing, and have lost my kingdom just the same. It was Smerdis the Magus, not my brother, of whose rebellion God warned me in my dream. Well—I did the deed, and you may be sure you will never see Smerdis the son of Cyrus again. You have the two Magi to rule you now: Patizeithes, whom I left in control of my household, and his brother Smerdis. The one man who of all others should have helped me against the shameful plot of the two Magi, has come to a horrid end at the hands of those nearest and dearest to him. But since he is dead, I must do that next best thing and tell you with my last breath what I would wish you to do. In the

Sesostris (Ramses II) makes an offering to Apis

name of the gods who watch over our royal house, the command I lay upon all of you, and especially upon those of the Achaemenidae who are here present, is this: do not allow the dominion to pass again into the hands of the Medes. If they have won it by treachery, with the same weapon take it from them; if by force, then play the man and by force recover it. If you do as I bid you, I pray that the earth may be fruitful for you, your wives bear you children, your flocks multiply and freedom be yours for ever: but if you fail to recover, or make no attempt to recover, the sovereign power, then my curse be upon you—may your fate be just the opposite, and, in addition to that, may every Persian perish as miserably as I.' Having said this, Cambyses bitterly lamented the cruelty of his lot, and when the Persians saw the king in tears, they tore their clothes, and showed their sympathy by a great deal of crying and groaning. Shortly afterwards gangrene and mortification of the thigh set in, and Cambyses died, after a reign in all of seven years and five months. He had no children, either sons or daughters.

The first person to suspect that the ruler was not the son of Cyrus but an imposter, was a certain Otanes, the son of Pharnaspes, one of the wealthiest members of the Persian nobility, and his suspicions were aroused by the fact that Smerdis never ventured outside the central fortifications of the capital, and never summoned any eminent Persians to a private audience.

Otanes asked his daughter Phaideme, who was one of the royal wives, to feel in the dark for the ears of her husband. Since he had no ears, then he was Smerdis the Magus, who had been punished for a crime by Cyrus by having his ears cut off.

Otanes took into his confidence Aspathines and Gobryas, two eminent Persians whom he had special reason to trust, and told them of his discovery. Both these men already had their suspicions of the truth, and were ready enough, in consequence, to accept what Otanes said, and it was then agreed that each of the three should choose his most trustworthy friend and bring him in as an accomplice. Otanes chose Intaphrenes, Gobryas Megabyzus, and Aspathines Hydarnes. The number of conspirators was thus raised to six, and on the arrival at Susa from Persia of Darius, whose father Hystaspes was governor there, it was decided to add him to the number.

Otanes wanted to delay the attack, but Darius was adamant about doing it immediately.

'Otanes,' Darius answered, 'there are many occasions when words are useless, and only deeds will make a man's meaning plain; often enough, too, it is easy to talk—and only to talk, for no brave act follows. You know there will be no difficulty in passing the guards. Who will dare to refuse admission to men of our rank and distinction, if not from respect, then from fear of the consequences? Besides, I have a perfect excuse for getting us in: I will say I have just come from Persia and have a message from my father for the king. If a lie is necessary, why not speak it? We are all after the same thing, whether we lie or speak the truth: our own advantage. Men lie when they think to profit by deception, and tell the truth for the same reason—to get something they want, and to be the better trusted for their honesty. It is only two different roads to the same goal. Were there no question of advantage, the honest man would be as likely to lie as the liar is, and the liar would tell the truth as readily as the honest man. Any sentry who lets us through without question, will be rewarded later; anyone who tries to stop us must be treated instantly as an enemy. We must force our way past him and set to work at once.' The supporters of Otanes urged delay and the risk of making their attempt until things calmed down again; but Darius and his party were still for immediate action and opposed to any change of plan. The argument was growing hot, when they suddenly saw seven pairs of hawks chasing two pairs of vultures, which they tore at, as they flew, with both beak and claw. It was an omen: forthwith the plan of Darius was unanimously accepted, and with renewed confidence the seven men hurried on towards the palace. When they reached the gates, everything turned out just as Darius had foreseen: the sentries, out of respect for their exalted rank and having no suspicion of the real purpose of their visit, allowed them to pass without question—almost as if they were under the special protection of heaven.

When both the Magi had been killed, the confederates decapitated them, and ran out into the street, shouting and making a great noise, with the severed heads in their hands. The two wounded men (*Aspathines and Intaphrenes*) had been left behind in the palace, being too weak to move—they were needed, moreover, to keep a watch upon the citadel. Once outside, the five who were unhurt appealed to their fellow citizens, told them what had happened, and showed them the heads—and then set about murdering every Magus they came across. The other Persians, once they had learnt of the exploit of the seven confederates, and understood the hoax which the two brothers had practised on them, were soon ready to follow their example: they, too, drew their daggers and killed every Magus they could find—so that if darkness had not put an end to the slaughter, the whole caste would have been exterminated. The anniversary of this day has become a red-letter day in the Persian calendar, marked by an important festival known as the Magophonia, or Killing of the Magi, during which no Magus is allowed to show himself—every member of the caste stays indoors till the day is over.

Five days later, when the excitement had died down, the conspirators met to discuss the situation in detail. At the meeting certain speeches were made—some of our own countrymen refuse to believe they were actually made at all; nevertheless they were. The first speaker was Otanes, and his theme was to recommend the establishment in Persia of democratic government. 'I think,' he said, 'that the time has passed for any one man amongst us to have absolute power. Monarchy is neither pleasant nor good. You know to what lengths the pride of power carried Cambyses, and you have personal experience of the effect of the same thing in the conduct of the Magus. How can one fit monarchy into any sound system of ethics, when it allows a man to do whatever he likes without any responsibility or control? Even the best of men raised to such a position would be bound to change for the worse—he could not possibly see things as he used to do. The typical vices of a monarch are envy and pride; envy, because it is a natural human weakness, and pride, because excessive wealth and power lead to the delusion that he is something more than a man. These two vices are the root cause of all wickedness: both lead to acts of savage and unnatural violence. Absolute power ought, by rights, to preclude envy on the principle that the man who possesses it has also at command everything he could wish for; but in fact it is not so, as the behavior of kings to their subjects proves: they are jealous of the best of them merely for continuing to live, and take pleasure in the worst; and no one is readier than a king to listen to tale-bearers. A king, again, is the most inconsistent of men; show him reasonable respect, and he is angry because you do not abase yourself before his majesty; abase yourself, and he hates you for being a superserviceable rogue. But the worst of all remains to be said—he breaks up the structure of ancient tradition and law, forces women to serve his pleasure, and puts men to death without trial. Contrast with this the rule of the people: first, it has the finest of all names to describe it—*isonomy*, or equality before the law; and, secondly, the people in power do none of the things that monarchs do. Under a government of the people a magistrate is appointed by lot and is held responsible for his conduct in office, and all questions are put up for open debate. For these reasons I propose that we do away with the monarchy, and raise the people to power; for the state and the people are synonymous terms.'

Otanes was followed by Megabyzus, who recommended the principle of oligarchy in the following words: 'In so far as Otanes spoke in favour of abolishing monarchy, I agree with him; but he is wrong in asking us to transfer political power to the people. The masses are a feckless lot—nowhere will you find more ignorance or irresponsibility or violence. It would be an intolerable thing to escape the murderous caprice of a king, only to be caught by the equally wanton brutality of the rabble. A king does at least act consciously and deliberately; but the mob does not. Indeed how should it, when it has never been taught what is right and proper, and has no knowledge of its own about such things? The masses have not a thought in their heads; all they can do is to rush blindly into politics and sweep all before them like a river in flood. As for the people, then, let them govern Persia's enemies, not Persia; and let us ourselves choose a certain number of the best men in the country, and give *them* political power. We personally shall be amongst them, and it is only natural to suppose that the best men will produce the best policy.'

Darius was the third to speak. 'I support,' he said, 'all Megabyzus' remarks about the masses but I do not agree with what he said of oligarchy. Take the three forms of government we are considering—democracy, oligarchy and monarchy—and suppose each of them to be the best of its kind; I maintain that the third is greatly preferable to the other two. One ruler: it is impossible to improve upon that—provided he is the best man for the job. His judgement will be in keeping with his character; his control of the people will be beyond reproach; his measures against enemies and traitors will be kept secret more easily than under other forms of government. In an oligarchy, the fact that a number of men are competing for distinction in the public service cannot but lead to violent personal feuds; each of them wants to get to the top, and to see his own proposals carried; so they quarrel. Personal quarrels lead to open dissension, and then to bloodshed; and from that state of affairs the only way out is a return to monarchy—a clear proof that monarchy is best. Again, in a democracy, malpractices are bound to occur; in this case, however, corrupt dealings in government services lead not to private feuds, but to close personal associations, the men responsible for them putting their heads together and mutually supporting one another. And so it goes on, until somebody or other comes forward as the people's champion and breaks up the cliques which are out for their own interests. This wins him the admiration of the mob, and as a result he soon finds himself entrusted with absolute power—all of which is another proof that the best form of government is monarchy. To sum up: where did we get our freedom from, and who gave it us? Is it the result of democracy, or of oligarchy, or of monarchy? We were set free by one man, and therefore I propose that we should preserve that form of government, and, further, that we should refrain from changing ancient laws, which have served us well in the past. To do so would lead only to disaster.'

These were the three views set out in the three speeches, and the four men who had not spoken voted for the last. Otanes (who had urged equality before the law), finding the decision against him, then made another speech. 'My friends,' he said, 'it is clear that the king will have to be one of ourselves, whether we draw lots for it, or ask the people of Persia to make their choice between us, or use some other method. I will not compete with you for the crown, for I have no wish to rule—or to *be* ruled either. I withdraw, therefore, upon one condition: that neither I myself, nor any of my descendants, shall be forced to submit to the rule of that one of you, whoever he is, who becomes king.' The other six agreed to this condition, and Otanes stood down. To this day the family of Otanes continues to be the only free family in Persia, and submits to the king only so far as the members of it may choose; they are bound, however, to observe the law like anyone else.

The other six then discussed the fairest way of deciding who should have the throne. They agreed that, if it fell to any of themselves, Otanes and his descendants should receive, every year, a suit of Median clothes and such other gifts as are held to be of most value by the Persians, as a mark of honour for the part he had played in the plot against the Magi, of which he was the prime mover and principal organizer. These privileges were for Otanes only; they also agreed upon another to be shared by all: permission, namely, for any of the seven to enter the palace unannounced, except when the king was in bed with a woman. They further agreed that the king should not marry outside the families of the seven confederates. To choose which should be king, they proposed to mount their horses on the outskirts of the city, and he whose horse neighed first after the sun was up should have the throne.

Darius had a clever groom called Oebares. After the meeting had broken up, he went to see this fellow, and told him of the arrangement they had come to, whereby they should sit on their horses' backs and the throne should be given to the one whose horse neighed first as the sun rose. 'So if,' he added, 'you can think of some dodge or other, do what you can to see

A Persian guard

Bull, relief, Xerxes' Palace

that this prize falls to me, and to no one else.'

'Well, master,' Oebares answered, 'if your chance of winning the throne depends upon nothing but that, you may set your mind at rest; you may be perfectly confident—you, and nobody else, will be king. I know a charm which will just suit our purpose.'

'If,' said Darius, 'you really have got something which will do the trick, you had better hurry and get it all worked out. To-morrow is the day—so there is not much time.'

Oebares, accordingly, as soon as it was dark, took from the stables the mare which Darius' horse was particularly fond of, and tied her up

on the outskirts of the city. Then he brought along the stallion and led him round and round the mare, getting closer and closer in narrowing circles, and finally allowed him to mount her. Next morning just before dawn the six men, according to their agreement, came riding on their horses through the city suburb, and when they reached the spot where the mare had been tethered on the previous night, Darius' horse started forward and neighed. At the same instant, though the sky was clear, there was a flash of lightning and a clap of thunder: the double miracle was like a sign from heaven; the election of Darius was assured, and the other five leapt from their saddles and bowed to the ground at his feet.

In this way Darius became king of Persia. Following the conquests of Cyrus and Cambyses, his dominion extended over the whole of Asia, with the exception of Arabia. The Arabs had never been reduced to subjection by the Persians, but friendly relations had continued between the two countries ever since the Arabs let Cambyses pass through their territory on his Egyptian campaign; for without this service the invasion of Egypt would have been impracticable.

The first women Darius married were Cyrus' two daughters Atossa and Artystone; the former had previously been the wife of her brother Cambyses and also of the Magus; the latter was a virgin. Subsequently he married Parmys, a daughter of Cyrus' son Smerdis, and, in addition to these, the daughter of Otanes, the man who had exposed the Magus.

Democedes, a Greek doctor, became a favorite in Darius' court. He wanted to return to Greece and influenced Darius' wife Atossa to help.

The consequence was that in bed that night with Darius she began the following conversation: 'My lord, with the immense resources at your command, the fact that you are making no further conquests to increase the power of Persia, must mean that you lack ambition. Surely a young man like you, who is master of great wealth, should be seen engaged in some active enterprise, to show the Persians that they have a man to rule them. Indeed, there are two reasons for ending this inactivity: for not only will the Persians know their leader to be a man, but, if you make war, you will waste their strength and leave them no leisure to plot against you. Now is the time for action, while you are young; for as the body grows in strength, so does the mind; but as the years pass and the body weakens, the mind ages too and loses its edge.'

THE BATTLE AT MARATHON

FIGHTING *had been going on in Greece between the Spartans and the Athenians. Athens repelled the Spartans, attacked Chalcis, and took many prisoners, who were ransomed at two minae apiece.*

With a tenth of the ransom money they had a chariot-and-four made in bronze, and consecrated it as an offering to Athene. It is the first thing you see on the left as you pass through the Propylaea on the Acropolis. The inscription on it is as follows:

> Athens with Chalcis and Boeotia fought,
> Bound them in chains and brought their pride
>   to naught.
> Prison was grief, and ransom cost them dear—
> One tenth to Pallas raised this chariot here.

Thus Athens went from strength to strength, and proved, if proof were needed, how noble a thing freedom is, not in one respect only, but in all; for while they were oppressed under a despotic government, they had no better success in war than any of their neighbours, yet, once the yoke was flung off, they proved the finest fighters in the world. This clearly shows that, so long as they were held down by authority, they deliberately shirked their duty in the field, as slaves shirk working for their masters; but when freedom was won, then every man amongst them longed to distinguish himself.

Up to this period, the man who had exercised absolute power over (the Chersonese) was Miltiades, the son of Cimon and grandson of Stesagoras. He had inherited his position from Miltiades the son of Cypselus, who had come into possession of it in the following way. The Dolonci, a Thracian people to whom the Chersonese then belonged, finding themselves in difficulties in the war they were fighting with the Apsinthians, sent their chiefs to Delphi, to ask advice from the oracle. The Priestess replied by recommending them to take home with them, in order to resettle their affairs, the first man who, after they left the temple, should invite them to enter his house. The chiefs of the Dolonci, travelling by the Sacred Road, passed through Phocis and Boeotia, and then, as nobody asked them in, turned off and made for Athens.

Supreme power in Athens was at this time in the hands of Pisistratus, but a position of considerable importance was also enjoyed by Cypselus' son, Miltiades. Miltiades belonged to a family whose fortune was great enough to allow them to enter a four-horse chariot for the

The Parthenon

The Acropolis
from Hephaestus'
Temple

◄ Light over Vulcan's
temple

Games, and traced his descent back to Aeacus of Aegina; but further down the line his ancestry was Athenian, and Philaeus, the son of Ajax, was the first of the family to be naturalized in Athens. Now it happened that as the Dolonci passed his house, Miltiades, who was sitting in the porch, caught sight of them, and noticing that they were dressed like foreigners and carried spears, called out to them. The men came up to where he was sitting, whereupon he invited them in and offered them shelter and hospitality. The invitation was accepted, and, while they were staying in the house, they told

Miltiades all about the oracle, and then begged him to act upon the advice which God had given. Miltiades had no sooner heard their story than he agreed to do as they wished—for he disliked Pisistratus' government and was very willing to be out of the way. He lost no time, therefore, in going to Delphi, where he asked the oracle if he was right in acceding to the request which the Dolonci had made him. The Priestess replied in the affirmative, and the matter was settled: Miltiades, son of Cypselus—who before this time had won the four-horse chariot race at Olympia—collected

The winner

A chariot race

everybody in Athens who was willing to take part in the venture, and sailed with the Dolonci. He took possession of the country, and the chieftains who had brought him over got him established as supreme arbiter of the country's affairs.

Darius demanded gifts of earth and water from Athens, that is, signs of submission. The first major campaign by Persia against Athens was in progress under Mardonius, son-in-law of Darius. The fleet reached the area of Mt. Athos and the army captured Eretria.

From Thasos the fleet stood across to the mainland and proceeded along the coast to Acanthus, and from there attempted to double Athos; but before they were round this promontory, they were caught by a violent northerly gale, which proved too much for the ships to cope with. A great many of them were driven ashore on Athos and smashed up—indeed, report says that something like three hundred were wrecked, and over twenty thousand men lost their lives. The sea in the neighbourhood of Athos is full of man-eating monsters, so that those of the ships' companies who were not dashed to pieces on the rocks, were seized and devoured. Others, unable to swim, were drowned; others, again, died of cold.

While this terrible disaster was overtaking the fleet, on land Mardonius and his army in Macedonia were attacked in camp one night by the Brygi, a Thracian tribe. The Persian losses were heavy, and Mardonius himself was wounded. But in spite of their initial success the Brygi were not to escape a crushing blow; for Mardonius did not leave their country until he had brought them to complete submission.

This was the last act of the campaign; for the casualties his army had suffered by the attack of the Brygi, and the fearful losses of the fleet at Athos, now induced Mardonius to begin his retreat. The whole force, therefore, returned to Asia in disgrace.

Struggles continued throughout Greece. Athens and Aegina were at each other's throats.

Another campaign was undertaken by the Persians to conquer Greece. The fleet sailed through the Aegean Islands in order to avoid Mt. Athos. The destruction of Eretria was accomplished.

The Persian fleet sailed for Attica, everyone aboard in high spirits and confident that Athens would soon be given the same sort of medicine.

The part of Attic territory nearest Eretria—and also the best ground for cavalry to manoeuvre in—was at Marathon. To Marathon, therefore, Hippias directed the invading army, and the Athenians, as soon as the news arrived, hurried to meet it.

The Athenian troops were commanded by

Mount Athos

ten generals, of whom the tenth was Miltiades. Miltiades' father, Cimon the son of Stesagoras, had been banished from Athens by Pisistratus, the son of Hippocrates. While in exile he had the good fortune to win the chariot race at Olympia, thereby gaining the same distinction as his half-brother Miltiades. At the next games he won the prize again with the same team of mares, but this time waived his victory in favour of Pisistratus, and for allowing the latter to be proclaimed the winner was given a prom-

ise of safety and leave to return to Athens. At a later Olympic festival he won a third time, still with the same four mares. Soon after, Pisistratus having died, he was murdered by Pisistratus' sons, who sent some men to waylay him one night near the Council House. He was buried outside Athens, beyond what is called the Sunk Road, and opposite his grave were buried the mares which had thrice won the chariot race. This triple victory had once before been achieved by a single team, that of

Euagoras the Laconian; but there are no other instances of it. At the time of Cimon's death, Stesagoras, the elder of his two sons, was living in the Chersonese with Miltiades his uncle, and the younger son, who was called Miltiades after the founder of the settlement in the Chersonese, was with his father in Athens.

Before they left the city, the Athenian generals sent off a message to Sparta.

Athens asked Sparta to help repel the Persians.

'Men of Sparta' (the message ran) 'the Athenians ask you to help them, and not to stand by while the most ancient city of Greece is crushed and enslaved by a foreign invader. Already Eretria is destroyed, and her people in chains, and Greece is the weaker by the loss of one fine city.' The Spartans, though moved by the appeal, and willing to send help to Athens, were unable to send it promptly because they did not wish to break their law. It was the ninth day of the month, and they said they could not take the field until the moon was full. So they waited for the full moon, and meanwhile Hippias, the son of Pisistratus, guided the Persians to Marathon.

The previous night Hippias had dreamed that he was sleeping with his mother, and he supposed that the dream meant that he would return to Athens, recover his power, and die peacefully at home in old age. So much for his first interpretation. On the following day, when he was acting as guide to the invaders, he put the prisoners from Eretria ashore on Aegilia, an island belonging to the town of Styra, led the fleet to its anchorage at Marathon, and got the troops into position when they had disembarked. While he was busy with all this, he happened to be seized by an unusually violent fit of sneezing and coughing, and, as he was an oldish man, and most of his teeth were loose, he coughed one of them right out of his mouth. It

Miltiades' helmet

Beach at Marathon

fell somewhere in the sand, and though he searched and searched in his efforts to find it, it was nowhere to be seen. Hippias then turned to his companions, and said with a deep sigh: 'This land is not ours; we shall never be able to conquer it. The only part I ever had in it my tooth possesses.' So he had had to change his mind—and the meaning of the dream was now clear.

Amongst the Athenian commanders opinion was divided: some were against risking a battle, on the ground that the Athenian force was too small to stand a chance of success; others—and amongst them Miltiades—urged it. It seemed for a time as if the more faint-hearted

policy would be adopted—and so it would have been but for the action of Miltiades. In addition to the ten commanders, there was another person entitled to a vote, namely the polemarch, or War Archon, an official appointed in Athens not by vote but by lot. This office (which formerly carried an equal vote in military decisions with the generals) was held at this time by Callimachus of Aphidne. To Callimachus, therefore, Miltiades turned. 'It is now in your hands, Callimachus,' he said, 'either to enslave Athens, or to make her free and to leave behind you for all future generations a memory more glorious than ever Harmodius and Aristogeiton left. Never in the course of

63

Marathon battleground

our long history have we Athenians been in such peril as now. If we submit to the Persian invader, Hippias will be restored to power in Athens—and there is little doubt what misery must then ensue; but if we fight and win, then this city of ours may well grow to pre-eminence amongst all the cities of Greece. If you ask me how this can be, and how the decision rests with you, I will tell you: we commanders are ten in number, and we are not agreed upon what action to take; half of us are for a battle, half against it. If we refuse to fight, I have little doubt that the result will be the rise in Athens of bitter political dissension; our purpose will be shaken, and we shall submit to Persia. But if we fight before the rot can show itself in any of us, then, if God gives us fair play, we can not only fight but win. Yours is the decision; all hangs upon you; vote on my side, and our country will be free—yes, and the mistress of Greece. But if you support those who have voted against fighting, that happiness will be denied you—you will get the opposite.'

Miltiades' words prevailed. The vote of Callimachus the War Archon was cast on the right side, and the decision to fight was made.

The generals exercised supreme command in succession, each for a day; and those of them who had voted with Miltiades, offered, when their turn for duty came, to surrender it to him. Miltiades accepted the offer, but would not fight until the day came when he would in any case have had the supreme command. When it did come, the Athenian army moved into position for the coming struggle. The right wing was commanded by Callimachus—for it was the regular practice at that time in Athens that the War Archon should lead the right wing; then followed the tribes, one after the other, in an unbroken line; and, finally, on the left wing, was the contingent from Plataea. Ever since the battle of Marathon, when the Athenians offer sacrifice at their quadrennial festival, the herald links the names of Athens and Plataea in the prayer for God's blessing.

One result of the disposition of Athenian troops before the battle was the weakening of their centre by the effort to extend the line sufficiently to cover the whole Persian front; the two wings were strong, but the line in the centre was only a few ranks deep. The dispositions made, and the preliminary sacrifice promising success, the word was given to move, and the Athenians advanced at a run towards the enemy, not less than a mile away. The Persians, seeing the attack developing at the double, prepared to meet it confidently enough, for it seemed to them suicidal madness for the Athenians to risk an assault with so small a force—at the double, too, and with no support from either cavalry or archers. Well, that was what they imagined; nevertheless, the Athenians came on, closed with the enemy all along the line, and fought in a way not to be forgotten. They were the first Greeks, so far as I know, to charge at a run, and the first who dared to look without flinching at Persian dress and the men who wore it; for until that day came, no Greek could hear even the word Persian without terror.

The struggle at Marathon was long drawn out. In the centre, held by the Persians themselves and the Sacae, the advantage was with the foreigners, who were so far successful as to break the Greek line and pursue the fugitives inland from the sea; but the Athenians on one wing and the Plataeans on the other were both victorious. Having got the upper hand, they left the defeated Persians to make their escape, and then, drawing the two wings together into a single unit, they turned their attention to the Persians who had broken through in the centre. Here again they were triumphant, chasing the routed enemy, and cutting them down as they ran right to the edge of the sea. Then, plunging into the water, they laid hold of the ships, calling for fire. It was in this phase of the struggle that the War Archon Callimachus was killed, fighting bravely, and also Stesilaus, the son of Thrasylaus, one of the commanders; Cynegirus, too, the son of Euphorion, had his hand cut off with an axe as he was getting hold of a ship's stern, and so lost his life, together with many other well-known Athenians. Nevertheless the Athenians secured in this way seven ships; the rest managed to get off, and the

Temple of Poseidon

Persians aboard them, after picking up the Eretrian prisoners whom they had left on Aegilia, laid a course round Sunium for Athens, which they hoped to reach in advance of the Athenian army. In Athens the Alcmaeonidae were accused of suggesting this move; they had, it was said, an understanding with the Persians, and raised a shield as a signal to them when they were on board.

While the Persian fleet was on its way round Sunium, the Athenians hurried back with all possible speed to save their city, and succeeded in reaching it before the arrival of the Persians. Just as at Marathon the Athenian camp had been a plot of ground sacred to Heracles, so now they fixed their camp on another, also sacred to the same god, at Cynosarges. When the Persian fleet appeared, it lay at anchor for a while off Phalerum (at that time the chief harbour of Athens) and then sailed for Asia.

In the battle of Marathon some 6400 Persians were killed; the losses of the Athenians were 192.

After waiting for the full moon, two thousand Spartans set off for Athens. They were so anxious not to be late that they were in Attica on the third day after leaving Sparta. They had, of course, missed the battle; but such was their passion to see the Persians, that they went to Marathon to have a look at the bodies. That done, they complimented the Athenians on their good work, and returned home.

Apollo and a centaur

XERXES PLANS
TO CONQUER
GREECE

WHEN the news of the battle of Marathon reached Darius, son of Hystaspes and king of Persia, his anger against Athens, already great enough on account of the assault on Sardis, burst out still more violently, and he was more than ever determined to make war on Greece. Without loss of time he dispatched couriers to the various states under his dominion with orders to raise troops—and at a much higher rate than for the previous expedition; warships, transports, horses, and foodstuffs were also to be provided. So the royal command went round; Greece being the objective, all the best men were enrolled in the armies, preparations of all kinds were in full swing, and the whole continent was in uproar for the space of three years. In the year after that, a rebellion in Egypt, which had been conquered by Cambyses, served only to harden Darius' resolve to go to war, not only against Greece but against Egypt too.

Both expeditions were ready to start when a violent quarrel broke out between Darius' sons on the question of priority and succession; for according to Persian law the king may not march with his army until he has named his successor. Darius before his accession had three sons by his former wife, Gobryas' daughter, and four more after his accession by Atossa the daughter of Cyrus. The eldest of the first three was Artobazanes, and of the last four Xerxes. It was between these two, therefore, being sons of different mothers, that the dispute arose, Artobazanes basing his claim to the succession on the argument that he was the eldest of all Darius' sons and therefore, by universal custom, entitled to inherit his father's position, Xerxes urging in reply that he was the son of Atossa the daughter of Cyrus, who won the Persians their freedom.

Darius had not yet declared his mind, when Demaratus the son of Ariston arrived in Susa. Demaratus, it will be recalled, was the Spartan king who had been deposed and had afterwards gone into voluntary exile; and the story goes that when he heard about the dispute between Darius' sons, he went to see Xerxes and advised him to point out, in addition to the argument he was already using, that Darius was already on the throne of Persia when he was born, whereas Artobazanes was born before his father held any public office at all. It was therefore neither reasonable nor fair that the crown should pass to anyone but Xerxes. Even in Sparta, he went on to suggest, the custom was that if sons were born before the father came

A gold daric

to the throne, and another was born afterwards when he was king, the latter should succeed him. Xerxes adopted the suggestion and Darius, recognizing the justice of the argument, proclaimed him heir to the throne. Personally, I believe that even without this advice from Demaratus, Xerxes would have become king, because of the immense influence of Atossa.

Xerxes, then, was publicly proclaimed as next in succession to the crown, and Darius was free to turn his attention to the war. Death, however, cut him off before his preparations were complete; he died in the year following the Egyptian rebellion and the quarrel between his sons, after a reign of thirty-six years, and so was robbed of his chance to punish either his rebellious subjects or the Athenians. After his death the crown passed to his son Xerxes.

Xerxes began his reign by building up an army for a campaign in Egypt. The invasion of Greece was at first by no means an object of his

thoughts; but Mardonius—the son of Gobryas and Darius' sister and thus cousin to the king—who was present in court and had more influence with Xerxes than anyone else in the country, used constantly to talk to him on the subject. 'Master,' he would say, 'the Athenians have done us great injury, and it is only right that they should be punished for their crimes. By all means finish the task you already have in hand; but when you have tamed the arrogance of Egypt, then lead an army against Athens. Do that, and your name will be held in honour all over the world, and people will think twice in future before they invade your country.' And to the argument for revenge he would add that Europe was a very beautiful place; it produced every kind of garden tree; the land there was everything that land should be—it was, in short, too good for anyone in the world except the Persian king. Mardonius' motive for urging the campaign was love of mischief and adventure and the hope of becoming governor of Greece himself; and after much persistence he persuaded Xerxes to make the attempt.

After the conquest of Egypt, when he was on the point of taking in hand the expedition against Athens, Xerxes called a conference of the leading men in the country, to find out their attitude towards the war and explain to them his own wishes. When they met, he addressed them as follows: 'Do not suppose, gentlemen, that I am departing from precedent in the course of action I intend to undertake. We Persians have a way of living, which I have inherited from my predecessors and propose to follow. I have learned from my elders that ever since Cyrus deposed Astyages and we took over from the Medes the sovereign power we now possess, we have never yet remained inactive. This is God's guidance, and it is by following it that we have gained our great prosperity. Of our past history you need no reminder; for you know well enough the famous deeds of Cyrus, Cambyses, and my father Darius, and their additions to our empire. Now I myself, ever since my accession, have been thinking how not to fall short of the kings who have sat upon this throne before me, and how to add as much power as they did to the Persian empire. And now at last I have found a way to win for Persia not glory only but a country as large and as rich as our own—indeed richer than our own—and at the same time to get satisfaction and revenge. That, then, is the object of this meeting—that I may disclose to you what it is that I intend to do. I will bridge the Hellespont and march an army through Europe into Greece, and punish the Athenians for the outrage they committed upon my father and upon us. As you saw, Darius himself was making his preparations for war against these men; but death prevented him from carrying out his purpose. I therefore on his behalf, and for the benefit of all my subjects, will not rest until I have taken Athens and burnt it to the ground, in revenge for the injury which the Athenians without provocation once did to me and my father. These men, you remember, came to Sardis with Aristagoras the Milesian—a mere slave of ours—and burnt the temples, and the trees that grew about them; and you know all too well how they served our troops under Datis and Artaphernes, when they landed upon Greek soil. For these reasons I have now prepared to make war upon them, and, when I consider the matter, I find several advantages in the venture: if we crush the Athenians and their neighbours in the Peloponnese, we shall so extend the empire of Persia that its boundaries will be God's own sky. With your help I shall pass through Europe from end to end and make it all one country, so that the sun will not look down upon any land beyond the boundaries of what is ours. For if what I am told is true, there is not a city or nation in the world which will be able to withstand us, once Athens and Sparta are out of the way. Thus the guilty and the innocent alike shall bear the yoke of servitude.

'If, then, you wish to gain my favour, each

A gold Persian rhyton

Sesostris (Ramses II) conquered Europeans, Semites and Ethiopians

one of you must present himself willingly and in good heart on the day which I shall name; whoever brings with him the best equipped body of troops I will reward with those marks of distinction held in greatest value by our countrymen. Those are the orders I give you; nevertheless I am no tyrant merely to impose my will—I will throw the whole matter into open debate, and ask any of you who may wish to do so, to express his views.'

The first to speak after the king was Mardonius. 'Of all Persians who have ever lived,' he began, 'and of all who are yet to be born, you, my lord, are the greatest. Every word you have spoken is true and excellent, and you will not allow the wretched Ionians in Europe to make fools of us. It would indeed be an odd

thing if we who have defeated and enslaved the Sacae, Indians, Ethiopians, Assyrians, and many other great nations for no fault of their own, but merely to extend the boundaries of our empire, should fail now to punish the Greeks who have been guilty of injuring us without provocation. People of their race we have already reduced to subjection—I mean the Greeks of Asia, Ionians, Aeolians, and Dorians. Well then, my lord, who is likely to resist you when you march against them with the millions of Asia at your back, and the whole Persian fleet? Believe me, it is not in the Greek character to take so desperate a risk. But should I be wrong—should the courage born of ignorance and folly drive them to do battle with us, then they will learn that we are the best soldiers in

72

the world. Nevertheless, let us take this business seriously and spare no pains; success is never automatic in this world—nothing is achieved without trying.'

Xerxes' proposals were made to sound plausible enough by these words of Mardonius, and when he stopped speaking there was a silence. For a while nobody dared to put forward the opposite view, until Artabanus, taking courage from the fact of his relationship to the king—he was a son of Hystaspes and therefore Xerxes' uncle—rose to speak. 'My lord,' he said, 'without a debate in which both sides of a question are expressed, it is not possible to choose the better course. All one can do is to accept whatever it is that has been proposed. But grant a debate, and there is a fair choice to be made. We cannot assess the purity of gold merely by looking at it: we test it by rubbing it on other gold—then we can tell which is the purer. I warned your father—Darius my own brother—not to attack the Scythians, those wanderers who live in a cityless land. But he would not listen to me. Confident in his power to subdue them he invaded their country, and before he came home again many fine soldiers who marched with him were dead. But you, my lord, mean to attack a nation greatly superior to the Scythians: a nation with the highest reputation for valour both on land and at sea. It is my duty to tell you what you have to fear from them: you have said you mean to bridge the Hellespont and march through Europe to Greece. Now suppose—and it is not impossible—that you were to suffer a reverse by sea or land, or even both. These Greeks are said to be great fighters—and indeed one might well guess as much from the fact that the Athenians alone

Thundering Olympus

The Propylaea

destroyed the great army we sent to attack them under Datis and Artaphernes. Or, if you will, suppose they were to succeed upon one element only—suppose they fell upon our fleet and defeated it, and then sailed to the Hellespont and destroyed the bridge: then, my lord, you would indeed be in peril. I urge you, therefore, to abandon this plan; take my advice and do not run any such terrible risk when there is no necessity to do so. Break up this conference; turn the matter over quietly by yourself, and then, when you think fit, announce your decision. Nothing is more valuable to a man than to lay his plans carefully and well; even if things go against him, and forces he cannot control bring his enterprise to nothing, he still has the satisfaction of knowing that it was not his fault—the plans were well laid; if, on the other hand, he leaps headlong into danger and succeeds by luck—well, that's a bit of luck indeed, but he still has the shame of knowing that he was ill prepared.

'You know, my lord, that amongst living creatures it is the great ones that God smites with his thunder, out of envy of their pride. The little ones do not vex him. It is always the great buildings and the tall trees which are struck by lightning. It is God's way to bring the lofty low. Often a great army is destroyed by a little one, when God in his envy puts fear into the men's hearts, or sends a thunderstorm, and they are cut to pieces in a way they do not deserve. For God tolerates pride in none but Himself. Haste is the mother of failure—and for failure we always pay a heavy price; it is in delay our profit lies—perhaps it may not immediately be apparent, but we shall find it, sure enough, as times go on. Nevertheless, if there is no avoiding this campaign in Greece, I have one final proposal to make. Let the king stay here in Persia; and you and I will then stake our children on the issue, and you can start the venture with the men you want and as big an army as you please. Now for the wager: if the king prospers, as you say he will, then I consent that my sons should be killed, and myself with them; if my own prediction is fulfilled, *your* sons forfeit their lives—and you too—if you ever get home.

'Maybe you will refuse this wager, and still persist in leading an army into Greece. In that case I venture a prophecy: the day will come when many a man left at home will hear the news that Mardonius has brought disaster upon Persia, and that his body lies a prey to dogs and birds somewhere in the country of the Athenians or the Spartans—if not upon the road thither. For that is the way you will find out the quality of the people against whom you are urging the king to make war.'

Xerxes was exceedingly angry. 'Artabanus,' he replied, 'you are my father's brother, and that alone saves you from paying the price your empty and ridiculous speech deserves. But your cowardice and lack of spirit shall not escape disgrace: I forbid you to accompany me on my march to Greece—you shall stay at home with the women, and everything I spoke of I shall accomplish without help from you. If I fail to punish the Athenians, let me be no child of Darius, the son of Hystaspes, the son of Arsames, the son of Ariaramnes, the son of Teispes, the son of Cyrus, the son of Cambyses, the son of Teispes, the son of Achaemenes! I know too well that if we make no move, the Athenians will—they will be sure to invade our country. One has but to make the inference from what they did before; for it was they who marched into Asia and burnt Sardis. Retreat is no longer possible for either of us: if we do not inflict the wound, we shall assuredly receive it. All we possess will pass to the Greeks, or all they possess will pass to us. That is the choice before us; for in the enmity between us there is no middle course. It is right, therefore, that we should now revenge ourselves for the injury we once received; and no doubt in doing so I shall learn the nature of this terrible thing which is to happen to me, if I march against men whom Pelops the Phrygian, a mere slave of the Persian kings, once beat so soundly that to this very day both people and country bear the conqueror's name.'

However, Xerxes thought some more and almost gave up his plans to conquer Greece. But a dream in which a phantom figure urged him to war, on three successive nights, was interpreted by Magi as portending the conquest of the world by Persia. Xerxes assembled his army from every corner of the continent.

The army was indeed immense—far greater than any other in recorded history. It dwarfed the army Darius commanded on his Scythian campaign, and the great host of Scythians who burst into Media on the heels of the Cimmerians and brought nearly all upper Asia under their control; it was incomparably larger than the armies which the stories tell us Agamemnon and Menelaus led to Troy, or than those of the Mysians and Teucrians which before the Trojan War crossed the Bosphorus into Europe, overwhelmed Thrace and, coming down to the Adriatic coast, drove as far south as the river Peneus. All these armies together, with others like them, would not have equalled the army of Xerxes. There was not a nation in all Asia that he did not take with him against Greece; save for the great rivers there was not a stream his army drank from that was not drunk dry. Some nations provided ships, others formed infantry units; from some cavalry was requisitioned, from others transport vessels and crews to serve in them; from others, again, warships for floating bridges, or provisions and naval craft of various kinds.

On the previous occasion, it will be remembered, the Persian fleet came to grief in the attempt to round Mt Athos. In view of this, work had been going on here for the past three years or so to prevent a repetition of the disaster. A fleet of triremes lay at Elaeus in the Chersonese, and from this base men of the various nations of which the army was composed were sent over in shifts to Athos, where they were put to the work of cutting a canal under the lash. The natives of Athos were also forced to help dig. Bubares the son of Megabazus and Artachaees the son of Artaeus were the Persian officers in charge.

Everyone knows Mt Athos—that lofty promontory running far out into the sea. People live on it, and where the high land ends on the landward side it forms a sort of isthmus with a neck about a mile and a half wide, all of which is level, except for a few low hills, right

across from the coast by Acanthus to the other side near Torone. On this isthmus to the north of the high ground stands the Greek town of Sane, and south of it, on Athos itself, are Dium, Olophyxus, Acrothoon, Thyssus, and Cleonae—the inhabitants of which Xerxes now proposed to turn into islanders.

I will now describe how the canal was cut. A line was drawn across the isthmus from Sane and the ground divided into sections for the men of the various nationalities to work on. When the trench reached a certain depth, the labourers at the bottom carried on with the digging and passed the soil up to others above them, who stood on ladders and passed it on to another lot, still higher up, until it reached the men at the top, who carried it away and dumped it. Most of the people engaged in the work made the cutting the same width at the top as it was intended to be at the bottom, with the inevitable result that the sides kept falling in, and so doubled their labour. Indeed they all made this mistake except the Phoenicians, who in this—as in all other practical matters—gave a signal example of their skill. They, in the section allotted to them, took out a trench double the width prescribed for the actual finished canal, and by digging at a slope gradually contracted it as they got further down, until at the bottom their section was the same width as the rest.

In a meadow near by the workmen had their meeting-place and market, and grain ready ground was brought over in great quantity from Asia.

The Great Army started for Greece.

From the European shore Xerxes watched his troops coming over under the whips. The crossing occupied seven days and nights without a break. There is a story that some time after Xerxes had passed the bridge, a native of the country thereabouts exclaimed: 'Why, O God, have you assumed the shape of a man of Persia, and changed your name to Xerxes, in order to lead everyone in the world to the conquest and devastation of Greece? You could have destroyed Greece without going to that trouble.'

76

The army was well organized with contingents from all over Asia.

Over them, and in general command of the infantry, were Mardonius, the son of Gobryas, Tritantaechmes, the son of Artabanus (the man who voted against the campaign), Smerdomenes, the son of Otanes (both nephews of Darius and Xerxes' cousins), Masistes, the son Darius and Atossa, Gergis, the son of Ariazus, and Megabyzus, the son of Zopyrus. These six commanded all the infantry except the Ten Thousand—a body of picked Persian troops under the leadership of Hydarnes, the son of Hydarnes. This corps was known as the Immortals, because it was invariably kept up to strength; if a man was killed or fell sick, the vacancy he left was at once filled, so that the total strength of the corps was never less—and never more—than 10,000.

Of all the troops in the army the native Persians were not only the best but also the most magnificently equipped; their dress and armour I have mentioned already, but should add that every man glittered with the gold which he carried about his person in unlimited quantity. They were accompanied, moreover, by covered carriages full of their women and servants, all elaborately fitted out. Special food, separate from that of the rest of the army, was brought along for them on camels and mules.

Having sailed from one end to the other of the line of anchored ships, Xerxes went ashore again and sent for Demaratus, the son of Ariston, who was accompanying him in the march to Greece. 'Demaratus,' he said, 'it would give me pleasure at this point to put to you a few questions. You are a Greek, and a native, moreover, of by no means the meanest or weakest city in that country—as I learn not only from yourself but from the other Greeks I have spoken with. Tell me, then—will the Greeks dare to lift a hand against me? My own belief is that all the Greeks and all the other western peoples gathered together would be insufficient to withstand the attack of my army—and still more so if they are not united. But it is your opinion upon this subject that I should like to hear.'

'My lord,' Demaratus replied, 'is it a true answer you would like, or merely an agreeable one?'

'Tell me the truth,' said the king; 'and I promise that you will not suffer by it.' Encouraged by this Demaratus continued: 'My lord, you bid me speak nothing but the truth, to say nothing which might later be proved a lie. Very well then; this is my answer: poverty is my country's inheritance from of old, but valour she won for herself by wisdom and the strength of law. By her valour Greece now keeps both poverty and bondage at bay.

'I think highly of all Greeks of Dorian descent, but what I am about to say will apply not to all Dorians, but to the Spartans only. First then, they will not under any circumstances accept terms from you which would mean slavery for Greece; secondly, they will fight you even if the rest of Greece submits. Moreover, there is no use in asking if their numbers are adequate to enable them to do this; suppose a thousand of them take the field—then that thousand will fight you; and so will any number, greater than this or less.'

Xerxes laughed. 'My dear Demaratus,' he exclaimed, 'what an extraordinary thing to say! Do you really suppose a thousand men would fight an army like mine? Now tell me, would *you*, who were once, as you say, king of these people, be willing at this moment to fight ten men single-handed? I hardly think so; yet, if things in Sparta are really as you have described them, then, according to your laws, you as king ought to take on a double share—so that if every Spartan is a match for ten men of mine, I should expect you to be a match for twenty. Only in that way can you prove the truth of your claim. But if you Greeks, who think so much of yourselves, are all of the size and quality of those I have spoken with when they have visited my court—and of yourself, Demaratus—there is some danger of your words being nothing but an empty boast. But let me put my point as reasonably as I can— how is it possible that a thousand men, or ten thousand, or fifty thousand, should stand up to an army as big as mine, especially if they were

78

A sea of olives

not under a single master, but all perfectly free to do as they pleased? Suppose them to have five thousand men: in that case we should be more than a thousand to one! If, like ours, their troops were subject to the control of a single man, then possibly for fear of him, in spite of the disparity in numbers, they might show some sort of factitious courage, or let themselves be whipped into battle; but, as every man is free to follow his fancy, it is not conceivable that they should do either. Indeed, my own opinion is that even on equal terms the Greeks could hardly face the Persians alone. We, too, have this thing that you were speaking of—I do not say it is common, but it does exist; for instance, amongst the Persians in my body-guard there are men who would willingly fight with three Greeks together. But you know nothing of such things, or you could not talk such nonsense.'

'My lord,' Demaratus answered, 'I knew before I began that if I spoke the truth you would not like it. But, as you demanded the plain truth and nothing less, I told you how things are with the Spartans. Yet you are well aware that I now feel but little affection for my countrymen, who robbed me of my hereditary power and privileges and made me a fugitive without a home—whereas your father welcomed me at his court and gave me the means of livelihood and somewhere to live. Surely it is unreasonable to reject kindness; any sensible man will cherish it. Personally I do not claim to be able to fight ten men—or two; indeed I should prefer not even to fight with one. But should it be necessary—should there be some great cause to urge me on—then nothing would give me more pleasure than to stand up to one of those men of yours who claim to be a match for three Greeks. So it is with the Spartans; fighting singly, they are as good as any, but fighting together they are the best soldiers in the world. They are free—yes—but not entirely free; for they have a master, and that master is Law, which they fear much more than your subjects fear you. Whatever this master commands, they do; and his command never varies: it is never to retreat in battle, however great the odds, but always to

82

stand firm, and to conquer or die. If, my lord, you think that what I have said is nonsense—very well; I am willing henceforward to hold my tongue. This time I spoke because you forced me to speak. In any case, I pray that all may turn out as you desire.'

Xerxes was not at all angry with Demaratus' answer. He turned it off with a laugh and good-humouredly let him go.

Having received from Xerxes its orders to proceed, the fleet passed through the Athos canal, which led to the deep bight on which stand the towns of Assa, Pilorus, Singus, and Sarte; from all these places reinforcements were taken on board, and a course was set for the Gulf of Therma. Rounding Ampelus in Torone, some of the ships sailed up the bight past the towns of Torone, Galepsus, Sermyle, Mecyberna, and Olynthus in order to requisition more ships and men; but the main body of the fleet sailed direct from Cape Ampelus to Canastraeum (the southernmost point of Pallene), and then took over more reinforcements in both ships and men from Potidaea, Aphytis, Nea, Aege, Therambo, Scione, Mende, and Sane—all towns in what is now called Pallene, but used to be called Phlegra.

At Therma Xerxes halted his army, and the troops went into camp. There were so many of them that they occupied the whole seaboard from Therma in Mygdonia to the Lydias and Haliacmon—two rivers which unite and form the boundary between Bottiaeis and Macedonia. While they were encamped here, all the rivers I have mentioned supplied enough water for their needs except the Echeidorus, which was drunk dry.

Xerxes could see from Therma the Thessalian mountains—the towering peaks of Olympus and Ossa.

The purpose of Xerxes' expedition, which was directed nominally against Athens, was in fact the conquest of the whole of Greece. The various Greek communities had long been aware of this, but they viewed the coming danger with very different eyes. Some had already made their submission, and were consequently in good spirits, because they were sure of get-

Ancient olive tree

ting off lightly at the invaders' hands; others, who had refused to submit, were thrown into panic partly because there were not enough ships in Greece to meet the Persians with any chance of success, and partly because most of the Greeks were unwilling to fight and all too ready to accept Persian dominion.

The Persian forces continued southward.

The Athenians had sent their envoys to Delphi, and as soon as the customary rites were performed and they had entered the shrine and taken their seats, the Priestess Aristonice uttered the following prophecy:

> Why sit you, doomed ones? Fly to the world's
>   end, leaving
> Home and the heights your city circles like a
>   wheel.
> The head shall not remain in its place, nor the
>   body,
> Nor the feet beneath, nor the hands, nor the
>   parts between;
> But all is ruined, for fire and the headlong God
>   of War
> Speeding in a Syrian chariot shall bring you low.
> Many a tower shall he destroy, not yours alone,
> And give to pitiless fire many shrines of gods,
> Which even now stand sweating, with fear
>   quivering,
> While over the roof-tops black blood runs
>   streaming
> In prophecy of woe that needs must come. But
>   rise,
> Haste from the sanctuary and bow your hearts
>   to grief.

The Athenian envoys were greatly perturbed by this prophetic utterance; indeed they were about to abandon themselves to despair at the dreadful fate which the oracle declared was coming upon them, when Timon, the son of Androbulus and one of the most distinguished men in Delphi, suggested that they should re-enter the shrine with branches of olive in their hands and, in the guise of suppliants begging for a better fate, put their question a second time. The Athenians acted upon this suggestion and returned to the temple. 'Lord Apollo,' they said, 'can you not, in consideration of these olive boughs which we have brought you, give us some kindlier prophecy about our country? We will never go away until you do; indeed no: we'll stay here till we die.'

Thereupon the Prophetess uttered her second prophecy, which ran as follows:

> Not wholly can Pallas win the heart of
>   Olympian Zeus,
> Though she prays him with many prayers and
>   all her subtlety;
> Yet will I speak to you this other word, as firm
>   as adamant:
> Though all else shall be taken within the bound
>   of Cecrops
> And the gold of the holy mountain of Cithæron,
> Yet Zeus the all-seeing grants to Athene's
>   prayer
> That the wooden wall shall not fall, but help
>   you and your children.
> But await not the host of horse and foot coming
>   from Asia,
> Nor be still, but turn your back and withdraw
>   from the foe.
> Truly a day will come when you will meet him
>   face to face.
> Divine Salamis, you will bring death to women's
>   sons
> When the corn is scattered, or the harvest
>   gathered in.

This second answer seemed to be, as indeed it was, less menacing than the first; so the envoys wrote it down and returned to Athens. When it was made public upon their arrival in the city, and the attempt to explain it began, amongst the various opinions which were expressed there were two mutually exclusive interpretations. Some of the older men supposed that the prophecy meant that the Acropolis would escape destruction, on the grounds that the Acropolis was fenced in the old days with a thorn-hedge—the 'wooden wall' of the oracle; but others thought that by this expression the oracle meant ships, and they urged in consequence that everything should be abandoned in favour of the immediate preparation of a fleet. There was, however, for those who believed 'wooden wall' to mean ships, one disturbing thing—namely, the last two lines of the Priestess' prophecy:

The Delphian temple of Apollo

Salamis Island

Divine Salamis, you will bring death to women's
  sons
When the corn is scattered, or the harvest
  gathered in.

This was a very awkward statement and caused
profound disturbance amongst all who took
the wooden wall to signify ships; for the professional interpreters understood the lines to
mean that if they prepared to fight at sea, they

would be beaten at Salamis. There was, however, a man in Athens who had recently made a
name for himself—Themistocles, more generally known as Neocles' son; and he it was who
now came forward and declared that there was
an important point in which the professional
interpreters were mistaken. If, he maintained,
the disputed passage really referred to the
Athenians, it would not have been expressed

in such mild language. 'Hateful Salamis' would surely have been a more likely phrase than 'divine Salamis,' if the inhabitants of the island were really doomed to destruction. On the contrary, the true interpretation was that the oracle referred not to the Athenians but to their enemies. The 'wooden wall' did, indeed, mean ships; so he advised his countrymen to prepare at once to meet the invader at sea.

The Athenians found Themistocles' explanation of the oracle preferable to that of the professional interpreters, who had not only tried to dissuade them from preparing to fight at sea but had been against offering opposition of any sort. The only thing to do was, according to them, to abandon Attica altogether and seek a home elsewhere.

Once on a previous occasion Themistocles

Zeus

had succeeded in getting his view accepted, to the great benefit of his country. The Athenians from the produce of the mines at Laurium had amassed a large sum of money, which they proposed to share out amongst themselves at the rate of ten drachmas a man; Themistocles, however, persuaded them to give up this idea and, instead of distributing the money, to spend it on the construction of two hundred warships for use in the war with Aegina. The outbreak of this war at that moment saved Greece by forcing Athens to become a maritime power.

In point of fact the two hundred ships were not employed for the purpose for which they were built, and were consequently at the disposal of Greece in her hour of need. The Athenians also found it necessary to expand this existing fleet by laying down new ships, and they determined at a council, which was held after the discussion on the oracle, to take the god's advice and meet the invader at sea with all the force they possessed, and with any other Greeks who were willing to join them.

Representatives of the Greek states who

were loyal to the general cause now met for a conference. Guarantees were exchanged, and the decision was reached that the first thing to be done was to patch up their own quarrels and stop any fighting which happened to be going on amongst members of the confederacy. There were a number of such disputes at the time, the most serious being the quarrel between Athens and Aegina. Having learnt that Xerxes and his army had reached Sardis, they next resolved to send spies into Asia to get information about Persian movements; at the same time, in the hope of uniting, if it were possible, the whole Greek world and of bringing all the various communities to undertake joint action in face of the common danger, they decided to send an embassy to Argos to conclude an alliance, another to Gelo, the son of Dinomenes, in Sicily, and others, again, to Corcyra and Crete with appeals for help in the common cause. Gelo, by the way, was said to be very powerful—far more powerful than anyone else of Greek nationality.

These decisions were put into force at once. The private quarrels were made up, and three men sent off to Asia to collect information.

In Asia the men learned the might of Xerxes' forces. The Thessalians insisted that the Persians be stopped at the pass near Mt Olympus.

The Greek answer was to determine to send an army by sea to Thessaly, to defend the pass. The troops assembled and, after passing through the Euripus, came to Alus in Achaea, where they left the ships and proceeded to Thessaly on foot. Here they occupied Tempe, the pass which leads from lower Macedonia

Peneus River

into Thessaly along the Peneus, between Mt Olympus and Mt Ossa. It was here that some 10,000 Greek heavy infantry, reinforced by the Thessalian cavalry, took up their position. The Spartans were commanded by Euaenetus son of Carenus, who had been chosen for the post from the Polemarchs, though he was not of the royal blood; the Athenians were commanded by Themistocles, son of Neocles. The army had not been in Tempe many days when a message arrived from Alexander, the son of Amyntas, in Macedonia advising the Greek troops to withdraw, and adding an indication of the strength of the Persian army and fleet: the invaders, he assured them, would trample them to death if they stayed in the pass. The advice seemed to be sound, and was clearly offered by the Mace-donian in a friendly spirit, so the Greeks took it. I think myself that what persuaded them to go was the alarm they felt upon learning that there was another way into Thessaly through upper Macedonia and Perrhaebia, near Gonnus—the pass, in fact, by which Xerxes' army actually did come in.

The Greeks, then, re-embarked and returned to the Isthmus. Such were the circumstances of the expedition to Thessaly—it took place while Xerxes was at Abydos, just before he crossed the strait from Asia into Europe. The result of it was that the Thessalians, finding themselves without support, no longer hesitated but whole-heartedly worked in the Persian interest, so that in the course of the war they proved of the greatest use to Xerxes.

BATTLES OF THERMOPYLAE AND ARTEMISIUM

AFTER *returning to the Isthmus from Tempe, a conference was held. It was decided to try to stop the Persians at Thermopylae. This place, known for its hot springs, was near Artemisium where the army and navy could be in close communication. Here the distance from Mt. Oeta to the sea was only fifty feet and at Alpeni near by the space from the mountains to the sea was only a wagon track wide. The Phocians had built a wall on the mountains near by. It was assumed that there was no other way through Trachis to Greece except by this pass. Here the Greeks with their small numbers had the best chance of stopping the enormous Persian army.*

Xerxes continued moving southward.

The Persian fleet got as far as Sepias, and the army as far as Thermopylae, without loss. I find by calculation that their numbers up to this stage were as follows: first there was the fleet of 1207 ships belonging to the various nations which sailed from Asia, with its original complement of 241,400 men—allowing 200 to each ship. Each of these vessels carried, apart from native soldiers—or marines—and in addition to the crew, thirty fighting men who were either Persians, Medes, or Sacae, making an additional 36,210. Add to these the crews of the pente-

conters (50-oared galleys), carrying roughly 80 men apiece; there were, as I have already said, 3000 pentenconters, so this will make another 240,000. This was the naval force brought by Xerxes from Asia, and the total number of men aboard comes to 517,610.

As to the army, the infantry was 1,700,000 strong and the cavalry 80,000. Then there were the Arabian camel corps and the Libyan charioteers, which I reckon as a further 20,000. The grand total, therefore, of land and sea forces brought over from Asia was 2,317,610, excluding army servants and the men in the food transports. To this, moreover, must be added the troops which were collected as Xerxes passed through Europe. Here I must be content with a rough estimate. The Greeks of Thrace and of the islands off the coast furnished, I should say, 120 ships: this would make 24,000 men. The strength of the infantry furnished by the Thracians, Paeonians, Eordi, Bottiaei, Chalcidians, Brygi, Pierians, Macedonians, Dolopes, Magnetes, Achaeans, and the coastal settlements of Thrace, I would put at 300,000. So by adding these to the original force from Asia we get a total of 2,641,610 fighting men. Lastly, it is my belief that the army servants and camp followers, the crews of the provision boats and of other craft which sailed with the expedition were not less, but more, numerous than the actual fighting troops; however I will reckon them as neither more nor fewer, but as equal, and thus arrive at my final estimate, which is, that Xerxes, the son of Darius, reached Sepias and Thermopylae at the head of an army consisting, in all, of 5,283,320 men.

So much for the actual army and its attendants; as for eunuchs, female cooks, and soldiers' women, no one could attempt an estimate of their number, any more than of the various pack-animals and Indian dogs which followed the army. They were far too numerous to count. I am not surprised that with so many people

and so many beasts the rivers sometimes failed to provide enough water; what does surprise me is that the food never gave out, for I reckon that if no more than a quart of meal was the daily ration for one man, the total daily consumption would have amounted to 110,340 bushels—and this without counting what was consumed by the women, eunuchs, pack-animals, and dogs. Amongst all these immense numbers there was not a man who, for stature and noble bearing, was more worthy than Xerxes to wield so vast a power.

From Thessaly and Achaea Xerxes went on into Malis, following the coast of a bay in which there is a daily rise and fall of tide. The

Thermopylae hot springs

Phocian wall

Cliffs of Trachis

country round this bay is flat—broad in one part, very narrow in another; all round is a chain of lofty and trackless mountains, called the Cliffs of Trachis, which enclose the whole territory of Malis.

The position, then, was that Xerxes was lying with his force at Trachis in Malian territory, while the Greeks occupied the pass known locally as Pylae—though Thermopylae is the common Greek name. Such were the respective positions of the two armies, one being in control of all the country from Trachis northward, the other of the whole mainland to the south. The Greek force which here awaited the coming of Xerxes was made up of the following contingents: 300 heavy-armed infantry from Sparta, 500 from Tegea, 500 from Mantinea, 120 from Orchomenus in Arcadia, 1000 from other Arcadian towns; from Corinth there were 400, from Phlius 200, and from Mycenae 80. In addition to these troops from the Peloponnese, there were the Boeotian contingents of 700 from Thespiae and 400 from Thebes. The Locrians of Opus and the Phocians had also

Leonidas, King of Sparta

obeyed the call to arms, the former sending all the men they had, the latter one thousand. The other Greeks had induced these two towns to send troops by a message to the effect that they themselves were merely an advance force, and that the main body of the confederate army was daily expected; the sea, moreover, was strongly held by the naval forces, and under the control of Athens and Aegina. Thus there was no cause for alarm—for, after all, it was not a god who threatened Greece, but a man, and there neither was nor ever would be a man who was not born with a good chance of misfortune—and the greater the man, the greater the misfortune. The present enemy was no exception; he too was human, and was sure to be disappointed of his great expectations.

The appeal succeeded, and Opus and Phocis sent their troops to Trachis. The contingents of the various states were under their own officers, of whom the most generally respected was Leonidas the Spartan, and to him belonged the supreme command of the confederate army. Leonidas traced his descent directly back to Heracles, through Anaxandrides and Leon (his father and grandfather), Anaxander, Eurycrates, Polydorus, Alcamenes, Teleches, Archelaus, Agesilaus, Doryssus, Labotas, Echestratus, Agis, Eurysthenes, Aristodemus, Aristomachus, Cleodaeus—and so to Hyllus, who was Heracles' son. He had come to be king of Sparta quite unexpectedly, for as he had two elder brothers, Cleomenes and Dorieus, he had no thought of himself succeeding to the throne. Dorieus, however, was killed in Sicily, and when Cleomenes also died without an heir, Leonidas found himself next in the succession. He was older than Cleombrotus, Anaxandrides' youngest son, and was, moreover, married to Cleomenes' daughter. The three hundred men whom he brought on this occasion to Thermopylae were chosen by himself; they were all men in middle life and all fathers of living sons. He also took with him the Thebans I mentioned, under the command of Leontiades, the son of Eurymachus. The reason why he made a special point of taking troops from Thebes, and from Thebes only, was that the Thebans were

strongly suspected of Persian sympathies, so he called upon them to play their part in the war in order to see if they would answer the call, or openly refuse to join the confederacy. They did send troops, but their secret sympathy was nevertheless with the enemy. Leonidas and his three hundred were sent by Sparta in advance of the main army, in order that the sight of them might encourage the other confederates to fight and prevent them from going over to the enemy, as they were quite capable of doing if they knew that Sparta was hanging back; the intention was, when the Carneia was over (for it was that festival which prevented the Spartans from taking the field in the ordinary way) to leave a garrison in the city and join the confederate army with all the troops at their disposal. The other allied states proposed to act similarly; for the Olympic festival happened to fall just at this same period. None of them ever expected the battle at Thermopylae to be decided so soon—which was the reason why they sent only advance parties there.

The Persian army was now close to the pass, and the Greeks, suddenly doubting their power to resist, held a conference to consider the advisability of retreat. It was proposed by the Peloponnesians generally that the army should fall back upon the Peloponnese and hold the Isthmus; but when the Phocians and Locrians expressed their indignation at this suggestion, Leonidas gave his voice for staying where they were and sending, at the same time, an appeal for reinforcements to the various states of the confederacy, as their numbers were inadequate to cope with the Persians.

During the conference Xerxes sent a man on horseback to ascertain the strength of the Greek force and to observe what the troops were doing. He had heard before he left Thessaly that a small force was concentrated here, led by the Lacedaemonians under Leonidas of the house of Heracles. The Persian rider approached the camp and took a thorough survey of all he could see—which was not, however, the whole Greek army; for the men on the further side of the wall which, after its reconstruction, was now guarded, were out of sight. He did, none the less, carefully observe the troops who were stationed on the outside of the wall. At that moment these happened to be the Spartans, and some of them were stripped for exercise, while others were combing their hair. The Persian spy watched them in astonishment; nevertheless he made sure of their numbers, and of everything else he needed to know, as accurately as he could, and then rode quietly off. No one attempted to catch him, or took the least notice of him.

Back in his own camp he told Xerxes what he had seen. Xerxes was bewildered; the truth, namely that the Spartans were preparing themselves to kill and to be killed according to their strength, was beyond his comprehension, and what they were doing seemed to him merely absurd. Accordingly he sent for Demaratus, the son of Ariston, who had come with the army, and questioned him about the spy's report, in the hope of finding out what the unaccountable behaviour of the Spartans might mean. 'Once before,' Demaratus said, 'when we began our march against Greece, you heard me speak of these men. I told you then how I saw this enterprise would turn out, and you laughed at me. I strive for nothing, my lord, more earnestly than to observe the truth in your presence; so hear me once more. These men have come to fight us for possession of the pass, and for that struggle they are preparing. It is the common practice of the Spartans to pay careful attention to their hair when they are about to risk their lives. But I assure you that if you can defeat these men and the rest of the Spartans who are still at home, there is no other people in the world who will dare to stand firm or lift a hand against you. You have now to deal with the finest kingdom in Greece, and with the bravest men.'

Xerxes, unable to believe what Demaratus said, asked further how it was possible that so small a force could fight with his army. 'My lord,' Demaratus replied, 'treat me as a liar, if what I have foretold does not take place.' But still Xerxes was unconvinced.

For four days Xerxes waited, in constant expectation that the Greeks would make good their escape; then, on the fifth, when still they had made no move and their continued presence seemed mere impudent and reckless folly, he was seized with rage and sent forward the Medes and Cissians with orders to take them alive and bring them into his presence. The Medes charged, and in the struggle which ensued many fell; but others took their places, and in spite of terrible losses refused to be beaten off. They made it plain enough to anyone, and not least to the king himself, that he had in his army many men, indeed, but few soldiers. All day the battle continued; the Medes, after their rough handling, were at length withdrawn and their place was taken by Hydarnes and his picked Persian troops—the King's Immortals—who advanced to the attack in full confidence of bringing the business to a quick and easy end. But, once engaged, they were no more successful than the Medes had been; all went as before, the two armies fighting in a confined space, the Persians using shorter spears than the Greeks and having no advantage from their numbers.

On the Spartan side it was a memorable fight; they were men who understood war pitted against an inexperienced enemy, and amongst the feints they employed was to turn their backs in a body and pretend to be retreating in confusion, whereupon the enemy would come on with a great clatter and roar, supposing the battle won; but the Spartans, just as the Persians were on them, would wheel and face them and inflict in the new struggle innumerable casualties. The Spartans had their losses too, but not many. At last the Persians, finding that their assaults upon the pass, whether by divisions or by any other way they could think of, were all useless, broke off the engagement and withdrew. Xerxes was watching the battle from where he sat; and it is said that in the course of the attacks three times, in terror for his army, he leapt to his feet.

Next day the fighting began again, but with no better success for the Persians, who renewed their onslaught in the hope that the Greeks, being so few in number, might be badly enough disabled by wounds to prevent further resistance. But the Greeks never slackened; their troops were ordered in divisions corresponding to the states from which they came, and each division took its turn in the line except the Phocian, which had been posted to guard the track over the mountains. So when the Persians found that things were no better for them than on the previous day, they once more withdrew.

How to deal with the situation Xerxes had no idea; but while he was still wondering what his next move should be, a man from Malis got himself admitted to his presence. This was Ephialtes, the son of Eurydemus, and he had come, in hope of a rich reward, to tell the king about the track which led over the hills to Thermopylae—and the information he gave was to prove the death of the Greeks who held the pass.

Xerxes found Ephialtes' offer most satisfactory. He was delighted with it, and promptly gave orders to Hydarnes to carry out the movement with the troops under his command. They left camp about the time the lamps are lit.

The track begins at the Asopus, the stream which flows through the narrow gorge, and,

An athlete fixing his hair

running along the ridge of the mountain—
which, like the track itself, is called Anopaea—
ends at Alpenus, the first Locrian settlement as
one comes from Malis, near the rock known
as Black-Buttocks' Stone and the seats of the
Cercopes. Just here is the narrowest part of
the pass.

This, then, was the mountain track which
the Persians took, after crossing the Asopus.
They marched throughout the night, with the
mountains of Oeta on their right hand and
those of Trachis on their left. By early dawn
they were at the summit of the ridge, near the
spot where the Phocians, as I mentioned before,
stood on guard with a thousand men, to watch
the track and protect their country. The Phocians were ready enough to undertake this
service, and had, indeed, volunteered for it to
Leonidas, knowing that the pass at Thermopylae was held as I have already described.

*The Greeks received reports of the surprise
Persian movement and signs foretold by the
oracle. Leonidas dismissed all of the army
except the Spartans and Thespians (besides
the Thebans who were held as hostages).*

The prophecy was in hexameter verse and
ran as follows:

> Hear your fate, O dwellers in Sparta of the wide
>   spaces;
> Either your famed, great town must be sacked
>   by Perseus' sons,
> Or, if that be not, the whole land of Lacedaemon
> Shall mourn the death of a king of the house of
>   Heracles,
> For not the strength of lions or of bulls shall
>   hold him,
> Strength against strength; for he has the power
>   of Zeus,
> And will not be checked till one of these two he
>   has consumed.

I believe it was the thought of this oracle,
combined with his wish to lay up for the Spartans a treasure of fame in which no other city
should share, that made Leonidas dismiss those
troops; I do not think that they deserted, or
went off without orders, because of a difference
of opinion.

Prior to the battles at Thermopylae and

*Artemisium, considerable naval activity took
place. The Persian fleet, having reached Sepias,
anchored offshore. A heavy storm, then called a
Hellespontian, arose and caught the fleet. Four
hundred ships are said to have been lost with
great loss of treasure. After hearing the news,
the Greek fleet returned to Artemisium. The
Persian fleet went to Aphetae, a point in Magnesia. During the operation, fifteen ships were
separated from the main fleet and fell into
Greek hands.*

In the morning Xerxes poured a libation to
the rising sun, and then waited till about the
time of the filling of the market-place, when he
began to move forward. This was according to
Ephialtes' instructions, for the way down from
the ridge is much shorter and more direct than
the long and circuitous ascent. As the Persian
army advanced to the assault, the Greeks under
Leonidas, knowing that the fight would be their
last, pressed forward into the wider part of the
pass much further than they had done before;
in the previous days' fighting they had been
holding the wall and making sorties from behind it into the narrow neck, but now they left
the confined space and battle was joined on
more open ground. Many of the invaders fell;
behind them the company commanders plied
their whips, driving the men remorselessly on.
Many fell into the sea and were drowned, and
still more were trampled to death by their
friends. No one could count the number of the
dead. The Greeks, who knew that the enemy
were on their way round by the mountain track
and that death was inevitable, fought with
reckless desperation, exerting every ounce of
strength that was in them against the invader.
By this time most of their spears were broken,
and they were killing Persians with their
swords.

In the course of that fight Leonidas fell,
having fought like a man indeed. Many distinguished Spartans were killed at his side—their
names, like the names of all the three hundred,
I have made myself acquainted with, because
they deserve to be remembered. Amongst the
Persian dead, too, were many men of high distinction—for instance, two brothers of Xerxes,

The Asopus gorge ▶

Where Leonidas died

Habrocomes and Hyperanthes, both of them sons of Darius by Artanes' daughter Phratagune.

There was a bitter struggle over the body of Leonidas; four times the Greeks drove the enemy off, and at last by their valour succeeded in dragging it away. So it went on, until the fresh troops with Ephialtes were close at hand; and then, when the Greeks knew that they had come, the character of the fighting changed. They withdrew again into the narrow neck of the pass, behind the walls, and took up a position in a single compact body—all except the Thebans—on the little hill at the entrance to the pass, where the stone lion in memory of Leonidas stands to-day. Here they resisted to the last, with their swords, if they had them, and, if not, with their hands and teeth, until the Persians, coming on from the front over the ruins of the wall and closing in from behind, finally overwhelmed them.

The dead were buried where they fell, and with them the men who had been killed before those dismissed by Leonidas left the pass.

Over them is this inscription, in honour of the whole force:

Four thousand here from Pelops' land
Against three million once did stand.

The Spartans have a special epitaph; it runs:

Go tell the Spartans, you who read:
We took their orders, and are dead.

For the seer Megistias there is the following:

I was Megistias once, who died
When the Mede passed Spercheius' tide.
I knew death near, yet would not save
Myself, but share the Spartans' grave.

Such, then, is the story of the Greeks' struggle at Thermopylae. Xerxes, when the battle was over, summoned Demaratus to ask him some questions. 'Demaratus,' he began, 'you are a good man—the truth of your words proves it. Everything has turned out as you said it would. Now tell me—how many more Lacedaemonians are there? And how many of them are as good soldiers as these were? Or are they all as good?' 'Sire,' Demaratus answered, 'there are a great many men and many towns in Lacedaemon; but what you really want to know I will now tell you: there is in that country a town called Sparta, which contains about eight thousand men. All these are the equals of those who fought in this battle. The other men in Lacedaemon are not their equals—but good soldiers none the less.'

'Demaratus,' said Xerxes, 'tell me what you think would be the easiest way of defeating these people. You were once their king, so you must be well acquainted with all the ins and outs of their policy.'

'Sire,' replied Demaratus, 'if you are really serious in asking my advice, I am bound to tell you what I consider the best plan. Suppose you send three hundred ships from the fleet to Lacedaemon. Off the coast there is an island called Cythera—Chilon, the wisest man who ever lived amongst us, once said that it would be better for the Spartans if it were sunk beneath

The Lion of Cythera

Cape Artemisium

the sea, for he always expected that it would provide just such an opportunity for a hostile force as what I am now suggesting. It was not, of course, your attack that he foresaw—it was the prospect of any attack from any quarter that alarmed him. This, then, is my proposal: let your ships make Cythera their base, and from it spread terror over Lacedaemon. With a war of their own, on their own doorstep, as it were, you need not fear that they will help the other Greeks while your army is engaged in conquering them. Thus the rest of Greece will be crushed first and Lacedaemon will be left alone and helpless. On the other hand, if you decide against this plan, you may expect more trouble; for there is a narrow isthmus in the Peloponnese, and in it you will find all the troops from that part of Greece who have formed a league to resist you, and you will have to face bloodier battles than any you have yet witnessed. But if you take my advice, the Isthmus and the Peloponnesian towns will fall into your hands without a blow.'

At this point the conversation was interrupted by Achaemenes, Xerxes' brother and commander of the fleet, who happened to be present and was afraid Xerxes might be persuaded to adopt Demaratus' proposal. 'My lord,' he began, 'I see that you are allowing yourself to be influenced by a man who envies your success, and is probably a traitor to you. He is a typical Greek, and this is just how they love to behave—envying anyone else's good fortune and hating any power greater than their own. In our present circumstances, when we have already had four hundred ships wrecked, if you detach another three hundred from the fleet for a voyage round the Peloponnese, the enemy will be a match for us. Keep the fleet together, and they will never dare risk an engagement—the disparity in numbers will see to that; moreover, if fleet and army keep in touch and advance together, each can support the other; separate them, and you will be no more use to the fleet than the fleet to you. Only lay your own plans soundly, and you can afford not to worry about the enemy, or to keep wondering what they will do, how many they are, or

where they will elect to make a stand. They are quite capable of managing their own affairs, just as we are of managing ours. If the Spartans risk another battle with us, they will certainly not repair the injury they have already received.'

'Achaemenes,' Xerxes replied, 'I think you are right, and I will take your advice. Nevertheless, though Demaratus' judgement is not so good as yours, he told me in good faith what he thought best for me. I will not accept your suggestion that he is secretly hostile to my case; I have evidence of his loyalty in what he has said on previous occasions.'

After this conversation Xerxes went over the battlefield to see the bodies, and having been told that Leonidas was king of Sparta and commander of the Spartan force, ordered his head to be cut off and fixed on a stake. This is in my opinion the strongest evidence—though there is plenty more—that King Xerxes, while Leonidas was still alive, felt fiercer anger against him than against any other man; had that not been so, he would never have committed this outrage upon his body; for normally the Persians, more than any other nation I know of, honour men who distinguish themselves in war. However, Xerxes' order was carried out.

The Greek naval force was composed of 127 ships from Athens—partly manned by the Plataeans, whose courage and patriotism led them to undertake this service in spite of their ignorance of everything to do with the sea—40 from Corinth, 20 from Megara, 20 more from Athens manned by crews from Chalcis, 18 from Aegina, 12 from Sicyon, 10 from Sparta, 8 from Epidaurus, 7 from Eretria, 5 from Troezen, 2 from Styra, and 2—together with two fifty-oared galleys—from Ceos. Lastly, the Locrians of Opus contributed a squadron of seven galleys.

These, then, were the states which sent ships to Artemisium, and I have given the number which each contributed. The total strength of the fleet, excluding galleys, was thus 271 ships of war. The general officer in command, Eurybiades, the son of Eurycleides, was provided by

Sparta; for the other members of the confederacy had stipulated for a Lacedaemonian commander, declaring that rather than serve under an Athenian they would break up the intended expedition altogether. From the first, even before Sicily was asked to join the alliance, there had been talk of the advisability of giving Athens command of the fleet; but the proposal had not been well received by the allied states, and the Athenians waived their claim in the interest of national survival, knowing that a quarrel about the command would certainly mean the destruction of Greece.

The battles at sea around Artemisium ended in large losses for both the Greek and Persian sides.

After the battle both sides made all speed back to their moorings, and were not sorry to get there. The Greeks, once they were clear of the fighting, did, indeed, manage to possess themselves of the floating bodies and to salve the wreckage; nevertheless they had been so

Temple of Zeus

roughly handled—especially the Athenians, half of whose ships were damaged—that they determined to quit their station and withdraw further south.

While the Greeks were engaged in lighting the fires and slaughtering the cattle, the messenger arrived from Trachis. The Greeks had employed two scouts or messengers, to keep communication between the fleet and the army: at Artemisium Polyas, a native of Anticyra, kept a boat ready to report to the army at Thermopylae any reverse which might be suffered by the fleet, while the Athenian Abronichus, the son of Lysides, did similar duty with Leonidas, and had a thirty-oared galley always available to report to Artemisium, if the army got into any trouble. It was this Abronichus who now arrived with the news of the fate of Leonidas and his men. The effect was immediate; the Greeks put off their withdrawal not a minute longer, but got under way at once, one after another, the Corinthians leading, the Athenians bring up the rear.

After the battle at Thermopylae, men from the Persian fleet were taken sightseeing. Xerxes wanted to give the impression that a small number of Persians were killed, but the men were not fooled.

On the day after this, which had been spent in sight-seeing, the seamen rejoined their ships at Histiaea and the army with Xerxes set forward on its march. A few Arcadian deserters came in—men who had nothing to live on and wanted employment; they were taken to Xerxes and questioned about what the Greeks were doing. There was one Persian in particular who put the question, and he was told in reply that the Greeks were celebrating the Olympic festival, where they were watching athletic contests and chariot-races. When he asked what the prize was for which they contended, the Arcadians mentioned the wreath of olive-leaves which it is our custom to give. This drew from Tritantaechmes, the son of Artabanus, a remark which proved his true nobility of character—though it made Xerxes call him a coward; for when he learned that the prize was not money but a wreath, he could not help crying out in front of everybody, 'Good heavens, Mardonius, what kind of men are these that you have brought us to fight against—men who compete with one another for no material reward, but only for honour!'

SALAMIS

AFTER *leaving the Thermopylae area, part of the Persian army was directed toward Delphi.*

The news of the approach of the Persians caused consternation at Delphi; and in their terror the people asked the God's advice as to whether they should bury the sacred treasures or get them out of the country. The God replied that they were not to be disturbed, for he was well able to mount guard over his own property. This being decided, the Delphians began to think about saving themselves; first they sent their women and children across the water into Achaea, and then fled for refuge to the rocky summits of Parnassus, and stored their movable property in the Corycian cave, while a few of them made their escape to Amphissa in Locris. All abandoned the town except sixty men and the Priest of the oracle.

The Persians were now close at hand and within sight of the temple, when suddenly the Priest, whose name was Aceratus, saw weapons lying on the ground in front of the shrine—they were the sacred weapons which no human hand may touch, and they had been brought mysteriously out from their place within. He hastened to report this marvellous thing to the other Delphians who were still in the town.

Meanwhile the enemy were drawing quickly nearer, and when they reached the temple of Athene Pronaea even stranger things happened to them than what I have just recorded. It is surprising enough that weapons of war should move of their own accord and appear upon the ground outside the shrine; but what occurred next is surely one of the most extraordinary things ever known—for just as the Persians came to the shrine of Athene Pronaea, thunderbolts fell on them from the sky, and two pinnacles of rock, torn from Parnassus, came crashing and rumbling down amongst them, killing a large number, while at the same time there was a great cry from inside the shrine. All these things happening together caused a panic amongst the Persian troops. They fled; and the Delphians, seeing them on the run, poured down from their hiding-places in the mountains and attacked them with great slaughter. All who escaped with their lives made straight for Boeotia. There is a story, I am told, amongst those who got away, that there was yet another miraculous occurrence: they saw, so they said, two gigantic soldiers—taller than ever a man was—pursuing them and cutting them down. According to the Delphians, the mysterious warriors were Phylacus and Autonous, heroes

of old whose spirits protected their country. Both have enclosed plots of ground near the temple, which are held sacred to them—that of Phylacus lies along the road above the temple of Pronaea, and that of Autonous is near the spring of Castalia under the peak called Hyampia.

The rocks which fell from Parnassus were preserved until quite recently; they lay in the enclosure round the shrine of Pronaea, where they embedded themselves after crashing through the Persian troops. So now you know how it was that these people took their departure from the Holy Place at Delphi.

The Greek fleet, having sailed from Artemisium, brought up, at the Athenians' request, at Salamis. The Athenians' object in urging the commanders to take up this position was to give themselves an opportunity of getting their women and children out of Attica, and also of of discussing their next move—as their present circumstances, and the frustration of their hopes, most evidently demanded. They had expected that the full strength of the Peloponnesian army would concentrate in Boeotia to hold up the Persian advance, but now they found that nothing of the sort had happened; on the contrary, they learned that the Peloponnesians were concerned only with their own safety and were fortifying the Isthmus in order to protect the Peloponnese, while the rest of Greece, so far as they cared, might take its chance. It was this news which led to the request I spoke of, that the combined fleet should concentrate at Salamis.

While, therefore, the rest of the fleet lay at Salamis, the Athenians returned to their own harbours, and at once issued a proclamation that everyone in the city and countryside should get his children and all the members of his household to safety as best he could. Most of them were sent to Troezen, but some to Aegina and some to Salamis. The removal of their families was pressed on with all possible speed, partly because they wished to take the warning which had been given them by the oracle, but more especially for an even stronger reason. The Athenians say that the Acropolis is guarded by a great snake, which lives in the temple; indeed they believe so literally in its existence that every month they put out a honey-cake for it to eat. Now in the past the honey-cake used always to be consumed, but on this occasion it was untouched. The temple Priestess told them of this, and in consequence, believing that the goddess herself had abandoned the Acropolis, they were all the more eager to get clear of the town. As soon as everything was removed, they rejoined the fleet on its station.

When the commanders of the various contingents met at Salamis, a council of war was held, and Eurybiades called for suggestions, from anyone who wished to speak, on the most suitable place for engaging the enemy fleet: this, he said, would have to be in some part of Greece which was still under their control— Attica was excluded, as it had already been given up. The general feeling of the council was in favour of sailing to the Isthmus and fighting

The Acropolis snake

The Athenian treasury with trophy area

in defence of the Peloponnese, on the grounds that if they were beaten at Salamis they would find themselves blocked up in an island, where no help could reach them, whereas if disaster overtook them at the Isthmus, they could at least find refuge amongst their own people. This view was, of course, most strongly held by the Peloponnesian officers. While the discussion was still going on, a man arrived from Athens with the news that the Persians had entered Attica and that the whole country was ablaze. This was the work of the division of the army under Xerxes which had taken the route through Boeotia; they had burnt Thespia after the inhabitants had escaped to the Peloponnese, and Plataea too, and then entered Attica, where they were causing wholesale devastation. The Thebans had told them that Thespia

Castalia spring

and Plataea had refused to submit to Persian domination: hence their destruction. The march of the Persian army from the Hellespont to Attica had taken three months—and the actual crossing of the strait an additional one; it reached Attica during the magistracy of Calliades.

The Persians found Athens itself abandoned except for a few people in the temple of Athene Polias—temple stewards and needy folk, who had barricaded the Acropolis against the invaders with planks and timbers. It was partly their poverty which prevented them from seeking shelter in Salamis with the rest, and partly their belief that they had discovered the real meaning of the Priestess' oracle—that 'the wooden wall would not be taken.' The wooden wall, in their minds, was not the ships but the barricade, and that would save them.

The Persians occupied the hill which the Athenians call the Areopagus, opposite the Acropolis, and began the siege. The method they used was to shoot into the barricade arrows with burning tow attached to them. Their wooden wall had betrayed them, but still the Athenians, though in imminent and deadly peril, refused to give in, or even to listen to the proposals which the Pisistratidae made to them for a truce. All their ingenuity was employed in the struggle to defend themselves; amongst other things, they rolled boulders down the slope upon the enemy as he tried to approach the gates, and the device was so successful that for a long time Xerxes was baffled and unable to take them. It was a difficult problem for the Persians, but at last it was solved: a way of access to the Acropolis was found—and the prophecy fulfilled that all Athenian territory upon the continent of Greece must be overrun by the Persians.

There is a place in front of the Acropolis, behind the usual way up which leads to the gates, where the ascent is so steep that no guard was set, because it was not thought possible that any man would be able to climb it; here, by the shrine of Cecrops' daughter Aglaurus, a few soldiers managed to scramble up the precipitous face of the cliff. When the Athenians

saw them on the summit, some leapt from the wall to their death, others sought sanctuary in the inner shrine of the temple. The Persians made straight for the temple gates, flung them open and butchered every man who had hoped to find a refuge there. Having left not one of them alive, they stripped the temple of its treasures and destroyed the whole Acropolis by fire. Xerxes, now absolute master of Athens, despatched a rider to Susa with a letter for Artabanus announcing his success.

On the following day he summoned to his presence the Athenian exiles who were serving with the Persian forces, and ordered them to go up into the Acropolis and offer sacrifice there according to Athenian usage; possibly some dream or other had suggested this course to him, or perhaps his conscience was uneasy for the burning of the temple. The Athenian exiles did as they were bidden. I mention these details for a particular reason: on the Acropolis there is a spot which is sacred to Erechtheus—the 'earth-born,' and within it is an olive-tree and a spring of salt water. According to the local legend they were put there by Poseidon and Athene, when they contended for possession of the land, as tokens of their claims to it. Now it happened that this olive was destroyed by fire together with the rest of the sanctuary; nevertheless on the very next day, when the Athenians, who were ordered by the king to offer the sacrifice, went up to that sacred place, they saw that a new shoot eighteen inches long had sprung from the stump. They told the king of this.

Meanwhile at Salamis the effect of the news of what had happened to the Acropolis at Athens was so disturbing, that some of the naval commanders did not even wait for the subject under discussion to be decided, but hurried on board and hoisted sail for immediate flight. Some, however, stayed; and by these a resolution was passed to fight in defence of the Isthmus.

During the night, when the various commanders had returned on board after the break-up of the conference, an Athenian named Mnesiphilus made his way to Themistocles'

The Acrocorinth and Temple of Apollo

Acropolis olive tree

ship and asked him what plan it had been decided to adopt. On learning that they had resolved to sail to the Isthmus and to fight there in defence of the Peloponnese, 'No, no,' he exclaimed; 'once the fleet leaves Salamis, it will no longer be one country that you'll be fighting for. Everyone will go home, and neither Eurybiades nor anybody else will be able to prevent the total dissolution of our forces. The plan is absurd and will be the ruin of Greece. Now listen to me: try, if you possibly can, to upset the decision of the conference—it may be that you will be able to persuade Eurybiades to change his mind and remain at Salamis.'

Themistocles highly approved of this suggestion.

The conference met, and then, before Eurybiades even had time to announce its purpose, Themistocles, unable to restrain his eagerness, broke into a long and passionate speech. At last he was interrupted by Adeimantus, the son of Ocytus, commander of the Corinthian contingent. 'Themistocles,' he observed, 'in the races, the man who starts before the signal is whipped.' 'Yes,' was Themistocles' retort, 'but those who start too late win no prizes.' It was a mild retort—for the moment. To Eurybiades he used none of his previous arguments about the danger of the force breaking up if they left Salamis; for it would have been unbecoming to accuse any of the confederates actually to their faces. The line he took this time was quite different. 'It is now in your power,' he said, 'to save Greece, if you take my advice and engage the enemy's fleet here in Salamis, instead of withdrawing to the Isthmus as these other people suggest. Let me put the two plans before you, and you can weigh them up and see which is the better. Take the Isthmus first: if you fight there, it will have to be in the open sea, and that will be greatly to our disadvantage, with our smaller numbers and slower ships. Moreover, even if everything else goes well, you will lose Salamis, Megara, and Aegina. Again, if the enemy fleet comes south, the army will follow it; so you will yourself be responsible for drawing it to the Peloponnese, thus putting the whole of Greece in peril.

'Now for my plan: it will bring, if you adopt it, the following advantages: first, we shall be fighting in narrow waters, and that, with our inferior numbers, will ensure our success, provided things go as we may reasonably expect. The open sea is bound to help the enemy, just as fighting in a confined space is bound to help us. Secondly, Salamis, where we have put our women and children, will be preserved; and thirdly—for you the most important point of all—you will be fighting in defence of the Peloponnese by remaining here just as much as by withdrawing to the Isthmus—nor, if you have the sense to follow my advice, will you draw the Persian army to the Peloponnese. If we beat them at sea, as I expect we shall, they will not advance to attack you on the Isthmus, or come any further than Attica; they will retreat in disorder, and we shall gain by the preservation of Megara, Aegina, and Salamis—where an oracle has already foretold our victory. Let a man lay his plans with due regard to common sense, and he will usually succeed; otherwise he will find that God is unlikely to favour human designs.'

During his speech Themistocles was again attacked by the Corinthian Adeimantus, who told him to hold his tongue because he was a man without a country, and tried to prevent Eurybiades from putting any question to the vote at the instance of a mere refugee. Let Themistocles, he cried, provide himself with a country before he offered his advice. The point of the jibe was, of course, the fact that Athens had fallen and was in Persian hands. This time Themistocles' retort was by no means mild; he heartily abused both Adeimantus and the Corinthians, and made it quite plain that so long as Athens had two hundred warships in commission, she had both a city and a country much stronger than theirs—for there was not a single Greek state capable of repelling them, should they choose to attack.

With this he turned to Eurybiades again, and, speaking more vehemently than ever, 'As for you,' he cried, 'if you stay here and play the man—well and good; go, and you'll be the ruin of Greece. In this war everything depends upon the fleet. I beg you to take my advice; if you refuse, we will immediately put our families aboard and sail for Ciris in Italy—it has long been ours, and the oracles have foretold that Athenians must live there some day. Where will you be without the Athenian fleet? When you have lost it you will remember my words.'

This was enough to make Eurybiades change his mind; and no doubt his chief motive was apprehension of losing Athenian support, if he withdrew to the Isthmus; for without the Athenian contingent his strength would not have been adequate to offer battle. So he took the decision to stay where they were and fight it out at Salamis.

The skirmish of words was over; Eurybiades had made up his mind; and at once the ships' commanders began to prepare for action. Day broke; just as the sun rose the shock of an earthquake was felt both on land and at sea, and the Greeks resolved to offer prayers to the gods and to call upon the Sons of Aeacus to fight at their side. As they resolved, so they did: they prayed to all the gods, and called upon Ajax and Telamon there in Salamis, and sent a ship to Aegina for Aeacus himself and his Sons.

Meanwhile the Persian sailors had returned from Trachis to Histiaea after their sight-seeing tour of the battlefield, and three days later the fleet set sail. The ships passed through the Euripus, and in another three days arrived off Phalerum. In my judgement the Persian forces both by land and sea were just as strong at the time of their entry into Attica as they had been at Sepias and Thermopylae; for as an offset to the losses suffered in the storm, at Thermopylae, and at Artemisium, I reckon the reinforcements which had subsequently joined them. These were the Malians, Dorians, Locrians, and Boeotians, who took service under Xerxes with all the troops they had except the Thespians and Plataeans; and in addition to these they were further reinforced by the Carystians, Andrians, Tenians, and all the other island peoples except the five whom I mentioned above. At each forward step into Greece the Persians had received new accessions of men and ships.

All these troops came as far as Attica except the Parians, who had stayed behind in Cythnus to watch the course of the war; and the rest of the fleet arrived, as I have said, at Phalerum. Here Xerxes paid it a personal visit, because he wished to talk to the various commanding officers and to find out what they thought about the coming campaign; so when he had seated himself with all proper ceremony, the rulers of states and commanders of squadrons were summoned to appear before him, and took their seats according to the degree of privilege which the king had assigned them—the lord of Sidon first, the lord of Tyre second, and so on in their order. Then, as they sat there in order of rank, Xerxes sent Mardonius to ask the opinion of each one upon the propriety of risking a battle at sea. Mardonius accordingly went the round of the assembly and put his question, beginning with the lord of Sidon. The answers, with a single exception, were unanimously in favour of engaging the Greek fleet: the exception was Artemisia. 'Mardonius,' she said, 'tell the king for me that this is the answer I give—I, whose courage and achievements in the battles at Euboea were surpassed by none: say to him, "Master, my past services give me the right to advise you now upon the course which I believe to be most to your advantage. It is this: spare your ships and do not fight at sea, for the Greeks are infinitely superior to us in naval matters—the difference between men and women is hardly greater. In any case, what pressing need have you to risk further actions at sea? Have you not taken Athens, the main objective of the war? Is not the rest of Greece in your power? There is no one now to resist you—those who did resist have fared as they deserved. Let me tell you how I think things will now go with the enemy; if only you are not in too great a hurry to fight at sea—if you keep the fleet on the coast where it now is—then, whether you stay here or advance into the Peloponnese, you will easily accomplish your purpose. The Greeks will not be able to hold out against you for long; you will soon cause their forces to disperse—they will soon break up and go home. I hear they have no supplies in

The temple of Aphaea

Poseidon

the island where they now are; and the Peloponnesian contingents, at least, are not likely to be very easy in their minds if you march with the army towards their country—they will hardly like the idea of fighting in defence of Athens.

'"If, on the other hand, you rush into a naval action, my fear is that the defeat of your fleet may involve the army too. And there is one other point, my lord, to be considered: good

masters, remember, usually have bad servants, and bad masters good ones. You, then, being the best master in the world, are ill served: these people who are supposed to be your confederates—these Egyptians, Cyprians, Cilicians, Pamphylians—what a miserable lot they are!"'

Artemisia's friends were dismayed when they heard this speech, and thought that Xerxes would punish her for trying to dissuade him

120

from engaging the Greek fleet; but those who were jealous of her standing as the most privileged person in the forces were delighted at the prospect of her imminent execution. However, when the several answers to his question were reported to the king, he was highly pleased with Artemisia's; he had always considered her an admirable person, but now he esteemed her more than ever. Nevertheless his orders were that the advice of the majority should be followed, for he believed that in the battles off Euboea his men had shirked their duty because he was not himself present—whereas this time he had made arrangements to watch the fight with his own eyes.

The command was now given to put to sea, and the ships proceeded towards Salamis, where they took up their respective stations without interference from the enemy. It was late in the evening, with not enough light left to attack at once; so they prepared to go into action on the following day.

The Greeks were in a state of acute alarm, especially those from the Peloponnese: for there they were, waiting at Salamis to fight for Athenian territory, and certain, in the event of defeat, to be caught and blocked up in an island, while their own country was left without defence, and the Persian army that very night was on the march for the Peloponnese.

Nevertheless everything that ingenuity could contrive had been done to prevent the Persian army from forcing the Isthmus. On the news of the destruction of Leonidas' force at Thermopylae not a moment was lost; and troops from the various towns in the Peloponnese hurried to the Isthmus, where they took up their position under Cleombrotus, the son of Anaxandrides and brother of Leonidas. Their first act was to break up and block the Scironian Way; then, in accordance with a decision taken in council, they began work on a wall across the Isthmus. As there were many thousands there and every man turned to, it was soon finished. Stones, bricks, timbers, sandbaskets—all were used in the building, and the labour went on continuously night and day. The towns which sent men to help in this work

were the following: Sparta, all the towns in Arcadia, Elis, Corinth, Sicyon, Epidaurus, Phlius, Troezen, and Hermione: all these, in their overriding fear for the safety of Greece, sent every available man. The other Peloponnesian communities (though the Olympic and Carneian festivals were now over) remained indifferent.

The Greeks at the Isthmus, convinced that all they possessed was now at stake and not expecting any notable success at sea, continued to grapple with their task of fortification. The news of how they were employed nevertheless caused great concern at Salamis; for it brought home to everyone there not so much his own peril as the imminent threat to the Peloponnese. At first there was whipered criticism of the incredible folly of Eurybiades; then the smothered feeling broke out into open resentment, and another meeting was held. All the old ground was gone over again, one side urging that it was useless to stay and fight for a country which was already in enemy hands, and that the fleet should sail and risk an action in defence of the Peloponnese, while the Athenians, Aeginetans, and Megarians still maintained that they should stay and fight at Salamis.

At this point Themistocles, feeling that he would be outvoted by the Peloponnesians, slipped quietly away from the meeting and sent a man over in a boat to the Persian fleet, with instructions upon what to say when he got there. The man—Sicinnus—was one of Themistocles' slaves and used to attend upon his sons; some time afterwards, when the Thespians were admitting outsiders to citizenship, Themistocles established him at Thespia and made him a rich man. Following his instructions, then, Sicinnus made his way to the Persians and said: 'I am the bearer of a secret communication from the Athenian commander, who is a well-wisher to your king and hopes for a Persian victory. He has told me to report to you that the Greeks have no confidence in themselves and are planning to save their skins by a hasty withdrawal. Only prevent them from slipping through your fingers, and you have at this moment an opportunity of unparalleled success. They are at daggers drawn with each other, and will offer no opposition—on the contrary, you will see the pro-Persians amongst them fighting the rest.'

His message delivered, Sicinnus lost no time in getting away. The Persians believed what he had told them, and proceeded to put ashore a large force on the islet of Psyttaleia, between Salamis and the coast; then, about midnight, they moved one division of the fleet towards the western end of Salamis in order to encircle the enemy, while at the same time the ships off Ceos and Cynosura also advanced and blocked the whole channel as far as Munychia. The object of these movements was to prevent the escape of the Greek fleet from the narrow waters of Salamis, and there to take revenge upon it for the battles of Artemisium. The troops were landed on Psyttaleia because it lay right in the path of the impending action, and once the fighting began, most of the men and damaged vessels would be carried on to it, and could be saved or destroyed according as they were friends or enemies. These tactical moves were carried out in silence, to prevent the enemy from being aware of what was going on; they occupied the whole night, so that none of the men had time for sleep.

Now I cannot deny that there is truth in prophecies, and I have no wish to discredit them when they are expressed in unambiguous language. Consider the following:

When they shall span the sea with ships from
    Cynosura
To the holy shore of Artemis of the golden
    sword,
Wild with hope at the ruin of shining Athens,
Then shall bright Justice quench Excess, the
    child of Pride,
Dreadful and furious, thinking to swallow up
    all things.
Bronze shall mingle with bronze, and Ares with
    blood
Incarnadine the sea; and all-seeing Zeus
And gracious Victory shall bring to Greece the
    day of freedom.

With that utterance of Bacis in mind, absolutely clear as it is, I do not venture to say any-

thing against prophecies, nor will I listen to criticism from others.

The Greek commanders at Salamis were still at loggerheads. They did not yet know that the enemy ships had blocked their escape at both ends of the channel, but supposed them to occupy the same position as they had seen them in during the day. However, while the dispute was still at its height, Aristides came over in a boat from Aegina. This man, an Athenian and the son of Lysimachus, had been banished from Athens by popular vote, but the more I have learned of his character, the more I have come to believe that he was the best and most honourable man that Athens ever produced. Arrived at Salamis, Aristides went to where the conference was being held and, standing outside, called for Themistocles. Themistocles was no friend of his; indeed he was his most determined enemy; but Aristides was willing, in view of the magnitude of the danger which threatened them, to forget old quarrels in his desire to communicate with him. He was already aware of the anxiety of the Peloponnesian commanders to withdraw to the Isthmus; as soon, therefore, as Themistocles came out of the conference in answer to his call, he said: 'At this moment, more than ever before, you and I should be rivals; and the object of our rivalry should be to see which of us can do most good to our country. First, let me tell you that the Peloponnesians may talk as much or as little as they please about withdrawing from Salamis—it will make not the least difference. What I tell you, I have seen with my own eyes: they *cannot* now get out of here, however much the Corinthians or Eurybiades himself may wish to do so, because our fleet is surrounded. Go back to the conference, and tell them.'

'Good news and good advice,' Themistocles answered; 'what I most wanted has happened— and you bring me the evidence of your own eyes that it is true. It was I who was responsible for this move of the enemy; for as our men would not fight here of their own free will, it was necessary to make them, whether they wanted to do so or not. But take them the good news yourself; if I tell them, they will think I

122

have invented it and will not believe me. Please, then, go in and make the report yourself. If they believe you, well and good; if they do not, it's no odds; for if we are surrounded, as you say we are, escape is no longer possible.'

Aristides accordingly went in and made his report, saying he had come from Aegina and had been hard put to it to slip through the blockading enemy fleet, as the entire Greek force was surrounded. He advised them, therefore, to prepare at once to repel an attack. That said, he left the conference, whereupon another dispute broke out, because most of the Greek commanders refused to believe in the truth of Aristides' report. Nor were their doubts settled until a Tenian warship, commanded by Panactius, the son of Sosimenes, deserted from the Persian navy and came in with a full account of what had occurred. For this service the name of the Tenians was afterwards inscribed on the tripod at Delphi amongst the other states who

helped to defeat the invader. With this ship which came over to them at Salamis, and the Lemnian one which previously joined them at Artemisium, the Greek fleet was brought up to the round number of 380. Up till then it had fallen short of that figure by two.

Forced to accept the Tenians' report, the Greeks now at last prepared for action. At dawn the fighting men were assembled and Themistocles was chosen to address them. The whole burden of what he said was a comparison of the nobler and baser parts of human nature, and an exhortation to the men to follow the former in the coming ordeal. Then, having rounded off his speech, he gave the order for embarkation. The order was obeyed and, just as the men were going aboard, the ship which had been sent to Aegina to fetch the Sons of Aeacus, rejoined the fleet.

The whole fleet now got under way, and in a moment the Persians were on them. The Greeks

A trireme

Straits of Salamis

checked their way and began to back astern; and they were on the point of running aground when Ameinias of Pallene, in command of an Athenian ship, drove ahead and rammed an enemy vessel. Seeing the two ships foul of one another and locked together, the rest of the Greek fleet hurried to Ameinias' assistance, and the general action began. Such is the Athenian account of how the battle started; the Aeginetans claim that the first to go into action was the ship which fetched the Sons of Aeacus from Aegina. There is also a popular belief that the phantom shape of a woman appeared and, in a voice which could be heard by every man in the fleet, contemptuously asked if they proposed to go astern all day, and then cheered them on to the fight.

The Athenian squadron found itself facing the Phoenicians, who formed the Persian left wing on the western, or Salamis, side of the line; the Lacedaemonians faced the ships of Ionia, which were stationed on the Piraeus, or eastern, side. A few of the Ionians, but by no means the majority, remembered Themistocles' appeal and deliberately held back in the course of the fighting. The greater part of the Persian fleet suffered severely in the battle, the Athenians and Aeginetans accounting for a great many of their ships. The Persians were, indeed, bound to get the worst of it, because they were ignorant of naval tactics, and fought at random without any proper disposition of their force, while the Greek fleet worked together as a whole; none the less they fought well that day—far better than in the actions off Euboea. Every man of them did his best for fear of Xerxes, feeling that the king's eye was on him.

Xerxes watched the course of the battle from the base of Mt Aegaleos, across the strait from Salamis; whenever he saw one of his officers behaving with distinction, he would find out his name, and his secretaries wrote it down, together with his city and parentage.

When the Persian rout began and they were trying to get back to Phalerum, the Aeginetan squadron, which was waiting to catch them in the narrows, did memorable service. The enemy was in hopeless confusion; such ships as of-

fered resistance or tried to escape were cut to pieces by the Athenians, while the Aeginetans caught and disabled those which attempted to get clear of the strait, so that any ship which escaped the one enemy promptly fell amongst the other.

Such of the Persian ships as escaped destruction made their way back to Phalerum and brought up there under the protection of the army.

After the battle the Greeks towed over to Salamis all the disabled vessels which were adrift in the neighbourhood, and then prepared for a renewal of the fight, fully expecting that Xerxes would use his remaining ships to make another attack. Many of the disabled vessels and other wreckage were carried by the westerly wind to a part of the Attic coast called Colias, and in this way it came about that not only the prophecies of Bacis and Musaeus about this battle were fulfilled, but also another prophecy which had been uttered many years previously by an Athenian soothsayer named Lysistratus: the words of this one were, 'The Colian women shall cook their foods with oars.' The Greeks had forgotten about it at the time, but it was to happen, all the same, after Xerxes was gone.

Xerxes, when he realized the extent of the disaster, was afraid that the Greeks, either on their own initiative or at the suggestion of the Ionians, might sail to the Hellespont and break the bridges here. If this happened, he would be cut off in Europe and in danger of destruction. Accordingly, he laid his plans for escape; but at the same time, in order to conceal his purpose both from the Greeks and from his own troops, he began to construct a causeway across the water towards Salamis, lashing together a number of Phoenician merchantmen to serve at once for bridge and breakwater. He also made other preparations, as if he intended to fight again at sea. The sight of this activity made everybody confident that he was prepared to remain in Greece and carry on the war with all possible vigour; there was, however, one exception—Mardonius, who thoroughly understood how his master's mind worked and was in no way deceived. At the same time

Aegina Temple

Xerxes dispatched a courier to Persia with the news of his defeat.

There is nothing in the world which travels faster than these Persian couriers. The whole idea is a Persian invention, and works like this: riders are stationed along the road, equal in number to the number of days the journey takes—a man and a horse for each day. Nothing stops these couriers from covering their allotted stage in the quickest possible time—neither snow, rain, heat, nor darkness. The first, at the end of his stage, passes the dispatch to the second, the second to the third, and so on along the line, as in the Greek torch-race which is held in honour of Hephaestus. The Persian word for this form of post is *angarium*.

Mardonius could see that Xerxes took the defeat at Salamis very hard, and guessed that he had determined to get out of Athens. In these circumstances, as he was otherwise sure to be punished for having persuaded the king to undertake the expedition, he felt it would be better to renew the struggle in order either to bring Greece into subjection or, failing that, to die nobly in a great cause—though he naturally, preferred the former alternative. Accordingly, he approached Xerxes with a proposal. 'My lord,' he said, 'I beg you not to take recent events too deeply to heart. What are a few planks and timbers? The decisive struggle will not depend upon them, but upon men and horses. Not one of all these people who now imagine that their work is done, will dare leave his ship in order to oppose you, nor will the mainland Greeks—those who have done so already have paid the price. I suggest, therefore, an immediate attack upon the Peloponnese. Or wait a while, if you prefer. In any case do not lose heart; for the Greeks cannot possibly escape ultimate subjection. They will be brought to account for the injuries they have done you, now and in the past. That is your best policy; nevertheless I have another plan to offer, should you be determined to withdraw the army from Greece. My lord, do not give the Greeks the chance to laugh at us. None of the reverses we have suffered have been due to us— you cannot say that we Persians have on any occasion fought like cowards. Why should we care if the Egyptians and Phoenicians and Cyprians and Cilicians have disgraced themselves? Persia is not involved in their disgrace. No; it is not we who are responsible for what has occurred. Listen, then, to what I have to propose: if you have made up your mind not to stay here, then go home together with the greater part of the army, and I will make it my duty, with 300,000 picked troops, to deliver Greece to you in chains.'

The proposal was as welcome to Xerxes as

The Alpheos River

Themistocles ostracized

rescue to a drowning man; he was highly delighted, and told Mardonius that he would consider the two alternatives and let him know which he preferred to adopt. Accordingly he summoned a conference, and during the debate it occurred to him that it would be just as well to send for Artemisia to take part in the discussion, as she on a previous occasion had been the only one to give him sound advice. When she presented herself, Xerxes dismissed his Persian advisers, and all the guards, and addressed her in these words:

'Mardonius urges me to stay in Greece and attack the Peloponnese. According to him, my army and my Persian troops, who have not been responsible for any of our recent disasters, are anxious to prove their worth. His advice, therefore, is, either that I should undertake this campaign, or allow him to choose 300,000 men from the army and lead the expedition himself, while I return home with the remainder of my troops. With that force he promises to deliver Greece into my hands. You gave me good advice when you tried to dissuade me from risking the battle we have just fought at sea; so I would ask you to advise me now. Which of these two courses should I be wise to follow?'

'My lord,' Artemisia answered, 'it is not easy to give you the best advice; nevertheless, circumstances being as they are, I think that you should yourself quit this country and leave Mardonius behind with the force he asks for,

if that is what he wants, and if he has really undertaken to do as he has said. If his design prospers and success attends his arms, it will be *your* work, master—for your slaves performed it. And even if things go wrong with him, it will be no great matter, so long as you yourself are safe and no danger threatens anything that concerns your house. While you and yours survive, the Greeks will have to run many a painful race for their lives and land; but who cares if Mardonius comes to grief? He is only your slave, and the Greeks will have but a poor triumph if they kill him. As for yourself, you will be going home with the object of your campaign accomplished—for you have burnt Athens.'

Artemisia's advice was most agreeable to Xerxes, for it was the expression of his own thoughts. Personally, I do not think he would have stayed in Greece, had all his counsellors, men and women alike, urged him to do so—he was much too badly frightened. As it was, he complimented Artemisia and sent her off to Ephesus with his sons—some of his bastards which had accompanied him on the expedition.

Xerxes, having entrusted Artemisia with the duty of conducting his bastard sons to Ephesus, sent for Mardonius and told him to pick the troops he wanted, and to take care to make his deeds answer to his words. That day nothing further was done; but the same night the king gave his orders, and the fleet slipped away from

129

Phalerum, the commander of every vessel making the best speed he could across to the Hellespont, in order to guard the bridges for Xerxes' use on his return. Off Zoster, where some little rocky headlands run out from the coast, the Persians mistook the rocks for enemy ships and gave them a very wide berth; however, they realized their mistake after a time, and continued the voyage in company.

Meanwhile Themistocles, always greedy for money, sent demands to the other islands; he employed the same messengers as he had sent to Xerxes, and backed his demand by the threat that, if they did not pay what he asked, he would bring the Greek fleet and blockade them into surrender. By these means he succeeded in collecting large sums from the people of Carys-

tus and Paros, who took fright and paid up when they heard that Andros was already invested because of her support of Persia, and that Themistocles had the highest reputation of the Greek commanders. I cannot say whether or not any of the other islands gave Themistocles money—though they probably did. The Carystians got no benefit from their compliance; the Parians, however, fared better, for the money they gave apparently put Themistocles into a good temper, so that they escaped a visit from the fleet. Thus it was that Themistocles extorted money from the islands, while he lay at Andros. The other commanders knew nothing of these proceedings.

But later, despite his patriotism, Themistocles was eventually ostracized.

PLATAEA

AFTER *the battle at Salamis, Mardonius led his army to winter in Thessaly. Xerxes, meanwhile, escorted by an army of 60,000, returned to Asia. This army was led by Artybagus and returned to join Mardonius after Xerxes was safely in Persia.*

Meanwhile, the Greeks chose from the plunder "the first fruits to be offered to the Gods at Delphi, Sunium, and Salamis itself."

At Sparta, "wreaths of olive" prizes for valor were awarded to Themistocles and Eurybiades.

While in Thessaly, Mardonius chose Alexander of Macedon, son of Amyntas and related to the Persians by marriage, to be his ambassador to Athens.

On his arrival at Athens as Mardonius' ambassador, Alexander spoke in the following terms: 'Men of Athens, Mardonius wishes me to inform you that he has received a message from the king, to the effect that he is willing to forget all the injuries which Athens has done him. The king's orders to him are, first, to restore to Athens her territory, and, secondly, to allow her to choose in addition whatever other territory she wishes, and to enjoy her liberty. Let Athens but come to terms with the king, and he has his instructions to rebuild the tem-

ples which have been destroyed by fire. Those being the king's orders, he has no choice but to carry them out, unless you yourselves put obstacles in his way. "Why, then," Mardonius adds "are you so mad as to take arms against the king? You can never defeat him, and the time must come when you can resist him no longer. You have seen his army, its immense size, and what it is capable of doing; you know, too, how powerful a force I have at this moment in Greece. Even should you beat us—and, if you have any sense, you cannot hope to do so—another force many times as powerful will come against you. Stop imagining yourself a match for Xerxes: it can end only in the loss of your country and the continual peril of your lives. Come to terms with him instead—you have the finest possible opportunity of doing so, now that Xerxes is inclined that way. Make an alliance with us, frankly and openly, and so keep your freedom."

'So much for what Mardonius instructed me to say to you. Now let me speak for myself. There is no need to mention my goodwill towards you—that you already know well enough; I merely add my earnest entreaties that you will do as Mardonius asks. It is clear to me that you will not be able to maintain your struggle with Xerxes for ever—had I thought you could, I should never have come to Athens on this mission. But the fact is, Xerxes' power is superhuman, and his arm is long. If, then, you do not at once conclude a peace, now that such excellent terms are offered, I tremble for your future, when I think how of all the confederate states you lie most directly in the path of danger. Your country, being a sort of no-man's-land, is bound to be the scene of constant fighting, and again and again you will have to suffer alone. Do, therefore, what Mardonius urges; for surely it is no small thing that the king of Persia should single you out from all the people of Greece, and be willing to forgive the past and to become your friend.'

In Sparta the news of Alexander's visit to try to bring about an alliance between Persia and Athens caused consternation. The Spartans, remembering the prophecy that the Dorians would one day be expelled from the Peloponnese by the Persians and Athenians, and greatly fearing that the alliance might be concluded, at once decided to send representatives to Athens. It so happened that Alexander and the Spartan envoys had their audience at the same time; for the Athenians had dragged out their business with Alexander in the conviction that the Spartans would hear that someone had arrived in Athens to represent Persia in peace negotiations, and that the news would induce them to send representatives of their own without delay. So they deliberately protracted the discussions, in order that the Spartans might be present when they declared their views.

Accordingly, when Alexander had finished his speech, the Spartan envoys took up the tale to the following effect: 'The Spartans have sent us here to beg you not to endanger Greece by a departure from your previous policy, and to listen to no proposals from Persia. For any of the Greeks to do such a thing would be inconsistent with decency and honour; for you it would be far worse, for many reasons. It was you, in the first place, who started this war—our wishes were not considered. It began by being a war for your territories only—now all

Greece is involved. Again, it would be an intolerable thing that the Athenians, who for centuries past have been known so often as liberators, should now be the cause of bringing slavery upon Greece. We do, however, sympathize with you in the hardships you are forced to endure—the loss of two successive harvests and the ruin of your homes and property over so long a time; and in compensation we offer, in the name of Sparta and her allies, to provide support for all the women and other non-combatant members of your households, for as long as the war lasts.

'Do not let Alexander's smooth-sounding version of Mardonius' proposals seduce you; he does only what one might expect of him—a despot himself, of course he works in another despot's interest. But such conduct is not for you—at least, not if you are wise; for surely you know that in foreigners there is neither truth nor honour.'

The Athenians then gave Alexander their answer. 'We know,' it ran, 'as well as you do that the Persian strength is many times greater than our own: that, at least, is a fact which you need not have troubled to rub in. Nevertheless, such is our love of freedom, that we will defend ourselves in whatever way we can. As for making terms with Persia, it is useless to try to persuade us; for we shall never consent. You may tell Mardonius, therefore, that so long as the sun keeps his present course in the sky, we Athenians will never make peace with Xerxes. On the contrary, we shall oppose him unremittingly, putting our trust in the help of the gods and heroes whom he despised, whose temples and statues he destroyed with fire. Never come to us again with a proposal like this, and never think you are doing us good service when you urge us to a course which is contrary to all the dictates of religion and honour—for we have no wish that you, who are our friend and benefactor, should be treated here in a manner which would not be seemly for either of us.'

So much for the Athenians' answer to Alexander. To the Spartan envoys they said: 'No doubt it was natural that the Lacedaemonians should dread the possibility of our making terms with Persia; none the less it shows a poor estimate of the spirit of Athens. Were we offered all the gold in the world, and the fairest and richest country the earth contains, we should never consent to join the common enemy and bring Greece into subjection. There are many compelling reasons to prevent our taking such a course, even if we wished to do so: the first and greatest is the burning of the temples and images of our gods—now mere heaps of rubble. It is our bounden duty to avenge this desecration with all the power we possess—not to clasp in friendship the hand that wrought it. Again, there is the Greek nation—the common blood, the common language; the temples and religious ritual; the whole way of life we understand and share together—indeed, if Athens were to betray all this, it would not be well done. We would have you know, therefore, if you did not know it already, that we will never make peace with Xerxes so long as a single Athenian remains alive. We are deeply moved, however, by your kindness and thoughtfulness, and the offer you made to provide for our families in this time of distress. Nothing could be more generous; nevertheless we prefer to carry on as best we can, without being a burden to you. That being our resolve, get your army into the field with the least possible delay; for unless we are much mistaken, it will not be long before the enemy invades Attica—he will do it the instant he gets the news that our answer has been an absolute refusal of all his requests. This, then, is the moment for you to send a force to meet him in Boeotia, before he can appear in Attica.'

Athens had given her answer; and the Spartan envoys left for home.

When Alexander returned with the Athenian answer, Mardonius took his army and the Thebans and Thessalians to again destroy Athens. Upon reaching Attica, he found Athens deserted because help from the Peloponnese had not arrived.

The truth was, that just then it was the time of the Hyacinthia in Sparta, and the people were on holiday and thinking of nothing so much as of giving the God his due. It also hap-

pened that the wall they were building across the Isthmus was almost finished and about to receive the battlements along the top.

The Athenian messengers, accompanied by representatives from Megara and Plataea, reached Sparta in due course and obtained an audience with the Ephors. 'We have come,' they said, 'on behalf of the Athenians, to deliver the following message. The Persian king has offered to restore our country to us, and is willing, at the same time, not only to make an alliance with us on fair and equal terms, openly and honestly, but also to give us any other country we choose, in addition to our own. We, however, from our reverence of the God whom all Greece worships, and our revulsion from the very thought of treachery, peremptorily refused the offer, in spite of the fact that we ourselves have been basely betrayed by our own confederates, and are well aware that we should gain more by an agreement with Persia than by prolonging the war. None the less, we shall never willingly make terms with the enemy. Thus we, at any rate, pay our debts to Greece with no counterfeit coin; but you, who were in terror lest we should make peace with Persia, are ready to forget all about us now that you know without any doubt what stuff we are made of, and that we shall never be traitors to Greece—and now, too, that your fortification of the Isthmus is almost complete. You agreed with us to oppose the invader in Boeotia, but you broke your word and allowed him to invade Attica. This conduct on your part has roused the anger of Athens; for what you have done is unworthy of the hour and of yourselves. However, your immediate duty is to accede to our present request: put your army in the field, that you and we together may meet Mardonius in Attica. Now that Boeotia is lost to us, the best place to engage him, without our own territory, is the plain of Thria.'

After due consideration, 5,000 Spartan troops, each attended by seven helots, left for Athens. They were led by Pausanias, son of Calombrotus, who became the leader of all Greek forces.

The Argives, who had previously agreed

133

A running hoplite

with Mardonius to prevent Spartan troops
from taking the field, no sooner learned that
Pausanias' army had left Sparta than they
dispatched the best runner they could find with
a message to Attica. There he presented himself
to Mardonius, and said: 'I have been sent by
the Argives to tell you that the fighting force
of Lacedaemon is on the march, and that the
Argives have been powerless to stop it. You

must take measures accordingly.' The runner
then left for home, and Mardonius, having
heard his report, no longer felt inclined to
remain in Attica. Up till then he had held on
there before he wanted to find out which way
the Athenians would go, and in the hope that
they would come to terms he had refrained
throughout his stay from doing damage of any
kind to crops or property. Now, however, that

134

he had failed to win them over, and the whole position was clear, he withdrew from the district before Pausanias' force reached the Isthmus. Before he went, he burnt Athens and reduced to complete ruin anything that remained standing—walls, houses, temples, and all. His reason for abandoning Attica was that it was bad country for cavalry; moreover, had he been beaten in an engagement, his only way of retreat would have been by a narrow defile, which would have been held by a very small force. His plan, therefore, was to retire on Thebes, where he could fight in good cavalry country and with a friendly town in the neighbourhood.

More news now came that the Greek forces had concentrated in strength at the Isthmus, and Mardonius, in consequence, began his withdrawal by way of Decelea. The chief magistrates of the Boeotians had sent for men from the valley of the Asopus, and they acted as guides to the army, bringing it first to Sphendales and then on to Tanagra, where it halted for a night. Next day Mardonius made for Scolus, and so found himself in Theban territory. In spite of the fact that the Thebans were working in the Persian interest, he cut down all the trees in the neighbourhood—not, of course, as an act of hostility to Thebes, but simply for his own military needs, for he wished to construct a palisade to protect his troops and to have somewhere to retreat to in the event of the battle going against him. The position he occupied was along the Asopus, from Erythrae, past Hysiae, to the territory of Plataea; the palisade did not cover all this ground, but was approximately ten furlongs square.

While the Persian troops were working on the palisade, a Theban named Attaginus, the son of Phrynon, invited Mardonius and fifty other distinguished Persians to a banquet, for which he had made elaborate preparations. The banquet was held in Thebes, and all who were invited accepted the invitation. What I am about to relate, I heard from Thersander, a man greatly respected in his native town Orchomenus. Thersander told me that he himself had an invitation from Attaginus, and that amongst the guests there were, besides the Persians, fifty Thebans. At table, the two nationalities, Greek and Persian, were not kept separate, but on each couch there sat a Persian and a Theban, side by side. During the drinking which followed the banquet, the Persian who shared Thersander's couch asked him, in Greek, what town he came from. 'Orchomenus,' was the answer. 'Since you and I,' the Persian said, 'have eaten together at the same table and poured a libation from the same cup, I should like to leave you something by which you may remember the soundness of my judgement; thus you will be forewarned and be able to take proper measures for your own safety. You see these Persians at their dinner—and the army we left in camp over there by the river? In a short time from now you will see but a few of all these men left alive.' The Persian, as he spoke, wept copiously, and Thersander, greatly surprised at what he had said, answered: 'Are not Mardonius and the other high Persian officers under him the proper people to be told a thing like that?' 'My friend,' rejoined the other, 'what God has ordained no man can by any means prevent. Many of us know that what I have said is true; yet, because we cannot do otherwise, we continue to take orders from our commander. No one would believe us, however true our warning. The worst pain a man can have is to know much and be impotent to act.'

This tale, as I have said, I heard from Thersander of Orchomenus; he also told me that he repeated it soon after to various people before the battle of Plataea.

The Lacedaemonians halted at the Isthmus on their arrival there, and the other Peloponnesians who chose to do their duty—some had actually seen the Spartans on the march—felt ashamed to stay behind and take no part in the expedition. Accordingly, after getting favourable omens from the sacrifice, the combined forces of the Pelopennese left the Isthmus and advanced to Eleusis. Here they again offered sacrifice, and again getting good omens continued their advance, having now been joined by the Athenians, who had crossed to the mainland from Salamis. At Erythrae in Boeotia they learnt that the enemy had taken up his position on the Asopus, and, in view of this, themselves occupied the lower slopes of Cithaeron.

Now with expanded forces, both sides took battle positions. The Greeks stayed near the protection of the forested mountains and the Persians remained in open country where they could manoeuver with cavalry or fall back to the protection of Thebes.

There were many skirmishes and in one of them the distinguished Persian officer Masistus was killed. Since he was highly regarded, his death depressed the Persians greatly.

They moved from the region around Mt. Cithaeron to Plataea. The omens indicated to both sides that success lay only in defensive action, and therefore neither crossed the Asopus River.

More days of inactivity went by. Many Persians, including Artabazus, wanted to make gifts of value to the Greeks to end the hostilities.

Mardonius expressed himself in much more uncompromising terms, and had no intention whatever of agreeing with Artabazus. In his view, the right policy, as the Persian army was far stronger than the Greek, was to force an engagement at once, and not allow the enemy forces to increase any further; as for Hegesistratus and his sacrifice, it would be best to ignore them—certainly not to try to force their meaning—and to engage in battle in the good old Persian way. The proposal was carried without opposition—for it was Mardonius, not Artabazus, who held from Xerxes the command of the army. He then sent for his company commanders and the Greek officers who were serving under him, and asked if they knew of any prophecy which foretold the destruction of Persian troops in Greece. Nobody said a word: perhaps some of them were unaware of the prophecies, while others, who knew them well enough, felt it was safer not to mention them. Mardonius accordingly said: 'Either you know of no such prophecy, or are afraid to speak of it. Well, I *do* know of one, and I will tell it to you. It says that the Persians will come to Greece, sack the temple at Delphi, and then perish to a

man. Very well then: knowing that, we will keep away from the temple and make no attempt to plunder it—and thus avoid destruction. All of you, therefore, who wish your country well, may rejoice at this, and be very sure that we shall defeat the Greeks.' Thereupon he issued his orders to prepare for battle on the following day.

I happen to know that the oracle, which Mardonius applied to the Persians, actually referred to the Illyrians and the army of the Encheles; there are, however, some verses of Bacis which did, in fact, refer to this battle:

> By Thermodon and Asopus, where the grass
>   grows soft,
> Shall be gathering of Greeks and the sound of
>   strange tongues;
> And there beyond lot and portion many Medes
>   shall fall,
> Armed with the bow, when the day of doom
>   comes.

These verses, and other similar ones of Musaeus, I know referred to the Persians.

After Mardonius had asked his question about the oracles and spoken the words of encouragement which I mentioned, darkness fell and the watches were set. Some hours passed; and as soon as silence had descended on the two armies and the men all seemed to be asleep, Alexander, the son of Amyntas, the king and commander of the Macedonians, rode up to the Athenian guard-posts and asked permission to have a word with the officers in command. Most of the men on duty stayed at their posts, but a few of them hurried off and informed their officers that a man on horseback had arrived from the Persian army: he would say nothing, except that he wanted to speak to the officers in charge, whose names he mentioned. The Athenians at once accompanied the guards back to their post, and Alexander delivered his message. 'Men of Athens,' he said, 'I trust to your honour for what I am about to tell you: unless you wish to ruin me, you must keep it a secret from everybody except Pausanias. I should not be here at all if I had not at heart the common welfare of Greece—I am myself a Greek by descent, and have no wish

Plataea battleground

to see Greece exchange her freedom for slavery. Listen, then: Mardonius and his army cannot get satisfactory omens from their sacrifices— but for this, you would have been fighting long before now. Mardonius has decided, however, to ignore the omens and to attack at dawn. No doubt his anxiety to prevent still further reinforcements from reaching you has prompted his decision. Be ready for him, therefore. If, on the contrary, he should postpone his attack, my advice to you is to hold on where you are: for he has only a few days' supplies left.

'In the event of your bringing this war to a successful conclusion, you must remember me, and do something for my freedom: for the sake of Greece I have taken a great risk, in my desire to acquaint you with what Mardonius intends, and thus to save you from a surprise attack. I am Alexander of Macedon.'

This said, Alexander rode back to the camp

and resumed the position assigned to him, while the Athenian commanders hurried to Pausanias, on the right wing of the Greek army, and told him what they had just heard. Pausanias was much alarmed. 'As we are to be in action at dawn,' he said, 'we must alter our dispositions: you, with your Athenian troops, had better move over, in order to hold the attack of the Persian contingent, while the Spartans deal with the Boeotians and the other Greeks who now threaten your section of the line. Marathon gave you plenty of experience of Persian tactics—unlike us, who know nothing about them whatever. No Spartan here has ever been in action against Persian troops—but we are all familiar enough with the soldiers of Boeotia and Thessaly. So get moving at once, and come and take over the right wing. We will take your place on the left.'

'It occurred to us,' the Athenians replied, 'long ago—ever since we saw that your section would have to face the Persian thrust—to make the very suggestion which you have now been the first to put forward; but we were afraid of offending you. Now, however, that you have mentioned it yourselves, we willingly accept, and will do what you ask.'

The matter being settled to the satisfaction of both parties, at the first signs of dawn the Athenian and Spartan contingents changed places. The Boeotians, when they saw the movement, reported to Mardonius, and Mardonius immediately shifted his Persian troops to the other wing, so as still to face the Spartans. Pausanias, seeing that his own movement had not escaped the observation of the enemy, marched his men back again to the right wing—and, as before, Mardonius followed suit, so that Persians and Spartans were once again facing one another in their original positions. Mardonius then sent a herald to the Spartan lines. 'Men of Lacedaemon,' the message ran, 'everybody about here seems to think you are very brave. Everyone admires you for never retreating in battle and for never quitting your post: you stick to it, so they say, until death—either your enemy's or your own. But it turns out that all this is nonsense: for here you are, running away and deserting your post before the battle has even begun or a single blow been struck, and giving the place of danger to the Athenians, while you yourselves face men who are merely our slaves. This is by no means what brave men would do; indeed, we have been sadly mistaken about you. Your reputation led us to expect that you would send us a challenge, in your eagerness to match yourselves with none but Persian troops. We should have accepted the challenge, had you sent it; but you did not. We find you, instead, slinking away from us, as timid as deer. Well, as you have sent no challenge, we will send one ourselves: why should we not fight with equal numbers on both sides, with you (who are supposed to be the most valiant) as the champions of Greece, and ourselves as the champions of Asia? Then, if it seems a good thing that the rest should fight too, they can do so after we have finished; otherwise, let us settle it between us, and let the victor be considered to have won the battle for the whole army.'

The herald waited for a time after delivering this challenge; then, as nobody gave him an answer, he returned to Mardonius and told him what had happened. Mardonius was overjoyed and, in all the excitement of his empty victory, ordered his cavalry to attack. The Persian cavalry, being armed with the bow, were not easy to come to grips with; so when they moved forward against the Greek line they inflicted heavy losses with their arrows and javelins; they also choked up and spoilt the spring of Gargaphia, from which all the Greek troops got their water. Actually, only the Lacedaemonians were near the spring, the rest of the army being some distance away, in their various positions, but all close to the river Asopus; nevertheless they, too, had been forced to resort to the spring for water, because the enemy cavalry, with their missile weapons, prevented them getting it from the river. In these circumstances, their men being continually harassed by the Persian cavalry and cut off from their water, the commanders of the various Greek contingents went in a body to Pausanias on the right wing, to discuss these and other difficulties with him.

Lack of water, though bad enough, was by no means the only cause of distress: food, too, had run short, and the servants who had been sent to bring supplies from the Peloponnese had been stopped by parties of Persian cavalry and had failed to rejoin. In the course of the discussion it was agreed that, if the Persians let the day pass without bringing on a general engagement, they should shift their position to the Island—a tract of ground in front of Plataea, rather more than a mile from the Asopus and Gargaphia, where they then were. This place is a sort of 'island on land': there is a river which splits into two channels near its source on Cithaeron, and in the plain below the channels are about three furlongs apart, before they unite again further on. The name of the river is Oeroe, and it is known locally as 'the daughter of Asopus.' Two reasons led them to choose the Island for their new position: first, they would have an abundant supply of water; and, secondly, the enemy cavalry would be unable to hurt them. The plan was to make the move during the night, at the second watch, to prevent the enemy from observing them as they marched out, and thus to escape trouble from his cavalry on the way. It was further agreed that upon reaching the tract of land 'islanded' by the two channels of the Oeroe as it flows down from Cithaeron, they should detach, during the same night, one half of the army and send it into the hills of Cithaeron, to relieve the food convoys which were cut off there.

When Mardonius learned that the Greeks had slipped away under cover of darkness, and saw with his own eyes that not a man remained in the position they had previously held, he sent for Thorax of Larissa and his two brothers, Eurypylus and Thrasidaus. 'Well, gentlemen,' he exclaimed, 'what will you say, now that you see that place deserted? You, who are neighbours of the Lacedaemonians, used to tell me that they were grand fighters, and never ran away! Only yesterday you saw them try to get out of their place in the line, and now it is plain to all of us that last night they simply took to their heels and fled. Once they found it necessary to fight against troops which are, in actual

fact, first-rate, they showed clearly enough that there's nothing in them, and that their reputation was gained merely amongst Greeks—who have nothing in them either. Now *you* I can excuse for praising these men: you know nothing about the Persians—and you did know one or two things the Spartans have done; but I was much more surprised at Artabazus, that *he* should be frightened of the Lacedaemonians, and allow his fear to suggest to him the shameful policy of a general retreat within the fortification of Thebes, where we should stand a siege. I shall take care that the king is informed of that proposal of his—but that can wait; our immediate task is not to let the Greeks escape us by what they have done: they must be pursued till they are caught and punished for all the injuries they have inflicted upon us.'

So saying, Mardonius gave the order to advance. His men crossed the Asopus and followed at the double in the track of the Greek forces, who, it was supposed, were in full flight. Actually, it was the Spartans and Tegeans only that Mardonius was after, for the Athenians, who had marched by a different route across the level ground, were hidden from sight by the intervening hills.

When the officers of the other divisions of Mardonius' army saw the Persian contingent start in pursuit, they immediately ordered the standards to be raised, and all the troops under their command joined in the chase as fast as their legs would carry them. Without any attempt to maintain formation they swept forward, a yelling rabble, never doubting that they would make short work of the fugitives. Pausanias, when the enemy cavalry fell upon him, sent a rider to the Athenians with an appeal for help. 'Men of Athens,' the message ran, 'the great struggle is now upon us—the struggle which will determine the liberty or enslavement of Greece; but our friends fled last night from the field of battle and have betrayed us both. Now, therefore, our duty is plain: we must defend ourselves and protect each other as best we can. Had it been you who were first attacked by the Persian horse, we should have been bound to come to your assis-

The Gargaphian spring

tance, together with the Tegeans who are, like us, loyal to the cause of Greece; but as we, not you, are bearing the whole weight of the attack, it is your duty to support those companies which are hardest pressed. If you are in any difficulty which prevents you from coming to our aid, then send us your archers, and we shall be grateful. We acknowledge that throughout this war your zeal has been equalled by none; you will not, then, refuse this request.'

On receipt of this message the Athenians started to the relief of the Spartans, to whom they were anxious to give all the help they could; but they were no sooner on the move than they were attacked by the Greek troops under Persian command, who held the position facing them. The attack was a heavy one, and made it impossible for them to carry out

their purpose, so that the Lacedaemonians and Tegeans, whom nothing could induce to leave their side, were left to fight alone—the former 50,000 strong, including the light-armed auxiliaries, the latter 3000.

Once more, as they were about to engage with Mardonius and his men, they performed the ritual of sacrifice. The omens were not favourable; and meanwhile many of their men were killed, and many more wounded, for the Persians had made a barricade of their wicker shields and from the protection of it were shooting arrows in such numbers that the Spartan troops were in serious distress; this, added to the unfavourable results of the sacrifice, at last caused Pausanias to turn his eyes to the temple of Hera and to call upon the goddess for her aid, praying her not to allow the Greeks

The Plataea monument base

to be robbed of their hope of victory. Then, while the words were still upon his lips, the Tegeans sprang forward to lead the attack, and a moment later the sacrificial victims promised success. At this, the Spartans, too, at last moved forward against the enemy, who stopped shooting their arrows and prepared to meet them face to face.

The armies engaged first in a struggle for the barricade of shields; then, the barricade down, there was a bitter and protracted fight, hand to hand, close by the temple of Demeter. Again and again the Persians would lay hold of the Spartan spears and break them; in courage and strength they were as good as their adversaries, but they were deficient in armour, untrained, and greatly inferior in skill. Sometimes singly, sometimes in groups of ten men—perhaps fewer, perhaps more—they fell upon the Spartan line and were cut down. They pressed hardest at the point where Mardonius fought in person—riding his white charger, and surrounded by his thousand Persian troops, the flower of the army. While Mardonius was alive, they continued to resist and to defend themselves, causing, at the same time, many casualties in the Lacedaemonian ranks; but after his death, and the destruction of his personal guard—the finest of the Persian troops—the remainder yielded to the Lacedaemonians and took to flight. The chief cause of their discomfiture was their inadequate equipment: not properly armed themselves, they were matched against heavily armed infantry.

Thus the prophecy of the oracle was fulfilled, and Mardonius rendered satisfaction to the Spartans for the killing of Leonidas; and thus, too, Pausanias, son of Cleombrotus and grandson of Anaxandrides, won the most splendid victory which history records. Mardonius was killed by Arimnestus, a distinguished Spartan, who after the Persian wars met his own death, together with the three hundred men under his command, at Stenyclerus during a campaign against the entire forces of the Messenians.

Once their resistance was broken by the Lacedaemonians, the Persian troops fled in disorder and took refuge behind the wooden barricade which they had erected in Theban territory. It is a wonder to me how it should have happened that, though the battle was fought close to the holy precinct of Demeter, not a single Persian soldier was found dead upon the sacred soil, or even appears to have set foot upon it, while round about the temple, on unconsecrated ground, the greatest number were killed. My own view is—if one may have views at all about these mysteries—that the Goddess herself would not let them in, because they had burnt her sanctuary at Eleusis.

Artabazus appeared to be entering the battle but when he saw the Persians in flight, left for home.

Once the palisade was down, the Persians no longer kept together as an organized force; soldierly virtues were all forgotten; chaos prevailed and, huddled in thousands within that confined space, all of them were half dead with fright. To the Greeks they were such an easy prey that of the 300,000 men (excluding the 40,000 who fled with Artabazus) not 3000 survived. The Spartan losses in the battle amounted to 91 killed; the Tegeans lost 16, the Athenians 52.

Serving with the Aeginetans at Plataea there was a man named Lampon. His father was Pytheas, and he was a person of the highest distinction in his native town. This man went in a great hurry to see Pausanias, and made him a really shocking proposal. 'Son of Cleombrotus,' he said, 'the service you have already rendered is noble beyond all expectation. God has granted you the privilege of saving Greece and of winning for yourself the greatest name in history. Now, to crown all, there is one thing more that you should do, both to increase your own reputation and to make foreigners think twice in future before they offer insult and injury to the Greeks. When Leonidas was killed at Thermopylae, Xerxes and Mardonius had his head cut off and stuck on a pike: have your revenge, then; render like for like, and you will win the praise not only of every man in Sparta,

Demeter, Triptolemus and Persephone

Darius the Great King, written in Persian, Babylonian and Elamite

but of every man in Greece. Impale Mardonius' body, and Leonidas, your father's brother, will be avenged.'

Lampon really thought that this would be an acceptable suggestion; Pausanias, however, replied: 'I thank you, my Aeginetan friend, for your goodwill and concern for me; but, in regard to your judgement, you have failed to hit the mark. First, you exalt me and my country to the skies by your praise of my success; and then you would bring it all to nothing by advising me to insult a dead body, and by saying that my good name would be increased if I were to do a barbarous thing which no Greek could stoop to—a foul deed we shudder to see even savages commit. No, indeed; in this matter I hope I shall never please the Aeginetans, or anyone else who approves such beastliness. It is enough for me to please the Spartans, by reverence and decency in both word and deed.

As for Leonidas, whom you wish me to avenge, he is, I maintain, abundantly avenged already—surely the countless lives here taken are a sufficient price not for Leonidas only, but for all the others, too, who fell at Thermopylae. Never come to me with such a proposal again, and be grateful that you are allowed to go unpunished.' The rebuke was sufficient, and Lampon retired.

Pausanias now issued an order that everything of value which had fallen into their hands as a result of the battle should be collected by the helots, and that nobody else should touch it. The helots accordingly went over all the ground previously occupied by the Persians. Treasure was there in plenty—tents full of gold and silver furniture; couches overlaid with the same precious metals: bowls, goblets, and cups, all of gold; and waggons loaded with sacks full of gold and silver basins. From the bodies of the

144

dead they stripped anklets and chains and golden-hilted scimitars, not to mention richly embroidered clothes which, amongst so much of greater value, seemed of no account. Everything which the helots could not conceal—and that was a great deal—they declared to their superiors; but there was a great deal, too, which they stole and sold afterwards to the Aeginetans, who, by buying the gold at the price of brass (which the helots supposed it to be), laid the foundation of their future wealth.

When all the stuff had been collected, a tenth was set apart for the God at Delphi, and from this was made the gold tripod which stands next the altar on the three-headed bronze snake; portions were also assigned to the Gods of Olympia and the Isthmus, and from these were made, in the first case, a bronze Zeus, fifteen feet high and, in the second, a bronze Poseidon, nine and a half feet high. The rest of the booty—the Persians' women, pack-animals, gold, silver, and so on—was divided amongst the troops, every man receiving his due. There is no record of any special awards for distinguished service in the battle, but I imagine that they must have been made. Pausanias himself was granted ten of everything—women, horses, camels, and everything else.

A story has got about that Xerxes on his retreat from Greece left his tent with Mardonius. When Pausanias saw it, with its embroidered hangings and gorgeous decorations in silver

and gold, he summoned Mardonius' bakers and cooks and told them to prepare a meal of the same sort as they were accoustomed to prepare for their former master. The order was obeyed; and when Pausanias saw gold and silver couches all beautifully draped, and gold and silver tables, and everything prepared for the feast with great magnificence, he could hardly believe his eyes for the good things set before him, and, just for a joke, ordered his own servants to get ready an ordinary Spartan dinner. The difference between the two meals was indeed remarkable, and, when both were ready, Pausanias laughed and sent for the Greek commanding officers. When they arrived, he invited them to take a look at the two tables, saying, 'Gentlemen, I asked you here in order to show you the folly of the Persians, who, living in this style, came to Greece to rob us of our poverty.'

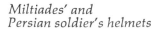

*Miltiades' and
Persian soldier's helmets*

APPENDIX

NOTE: *This page relates the abridged text to Herodotus' original. Since most translators take liberties with the original, there is some discrepancy between translated paragraphs and the original breaks. Pages with photographs and no text are not listed.*

Page	Book, Chapter	
1	I	1-2-3-4-5
2	I	8-9-10-11-12
3	I	12-13
4	I	13-14
5	I	31
8	I	31-32, 61, 108
9	I	108-119
10	I	120
11	II	4-5
15	II	10-11-20-21
16	II	21-28
17	II	29-31-35
20	II	35-36-37
21	II	35
23	II	40
27	II	40
29	II	41-60-64
30	II	65-66-68
31	II	71
32	II	78
33	II	79-86
34	II	92-93
37	II	96-97
38	II	99-111-124-125
39	II	125
40	II	126
41	II	127-128
42	II	129-131

Page	Book, Chapter	
43	II	145-148
44	II	149-160
46	II	172-174
47	III	1-27-28-64
48	III	68-70
49	III	72-76, 80
50	III	81-82, 83
51	III	83-84, 85
52	III	85-86-87, 88
53	III	88-134
55	{ V	77-78
	{ VI	34-35-36
58	VI	36
59	VI	36-44-47, 102-105
60	VI	105-106
61	VI	106-107
63	VI	107-108-109-110
65	VI	110-113-115
67	VI	115-117-120
69	VII	1-2-3
70	VII	4-5-6-7-8
71	VII	9
72	VII	9
73	VII	9
75	VII	10-11
76	VII	22-23-25-58
78	VII	86-101-102-103-104-105
82	VII	104-105-122-128-138
84	VII	140-141-142
86	VII	142-143-144
87	VII	145
88	VII	145-146
89	VII	173
90	VII	173-176
91	VII	178
92	VII	186-198
96	VII	204

Page	Book, Chapter	
97	VII	205-209
98	VII	209-210, 212-214
99	VII	214-215-216
100	VII	216-220, 223-226
102	VII	227-228
103	VII	228-234, 235
106	{ VII	235-236-237, 239
	{ VIII	1-2
107	VIII	2-18
108	VIII	21-27
109	VIII	36-37, 41
111	VIII	40-41-49
113	VIII	49
114	VIII	54-55, 56-57
117	VIII	57-58, 60-61-62-63
118	VIII	63-67, 70
120	VIII	70-71
121	VIII	71-76
122	VIII	77-79, 82-83
123	VIII	84
126	VIII	85-90, 94-97
127	VIII	100
128	VIII	100, 104
129	VIII	105-107-108
130	VIII	113
131	VIII	140-141-142
132	VIII	142-143, 144
133	{ VIII	144
	{ IX	8-14
134	IX	14
135	IX	14-15-17, 18-19
136	IX	43-44
137	IX	45-46
138	IX	48-49
139	IX	59-60
142	IX	62, 65, 66
144	IX	78-79-80
145	IX	81-82
146	IX	82-83

LOCATION OF PHOTOGRAPHS

Page

i Herodotus' Podium; Olympia, Greece.

ii–iii Broken gold Persian dagger; Metropolitan Museum of Art, New York.

ix Bust of Herodotus, Roman copy, found in Egypt; The Metropolitan Museum of Art, New York.

x Plains of Argos; Greece.

2 Helen and Menelaus; Sparta Museum, Greece.

3 A Persian servant, Xerxes Palace, Persepolis; Boston Museum of Fine Arts.

4 Cleobis and Biton; Delphi Museum, Greece.

5 Goddess Hera, Argos Heraion; The National Museum, Athens.

6–7 Temple of Hera; Argos, Greece.

8 Hippias; Acropolis Museum, Athens.

9 An Achaemenid vase, Leon Pomerance collection; The Metropolitan Museum of Art, New York.

12 Temple of Ptah; Memphis, Egypt.

13 Farming, a Nile canal; south of Giza, Egypt.

14 Pyramids of Mycerinus, Chephren and Cheops; Giza, Egypt.

14 Quarry for pyramids; east bank of Nile, north of Cairo.

15 Kites over the Nile, Luxor, Egypt.

16 Elephantine Island; Aswan, Egypt.

17 Defense wall; near Aswan, Egypt.

18–19 Wide Nile valley; south of Moqattam hills, Egypt.

20 Shaved priest; Egyptian Museum, Cairo.

21 Circumcision; a tomb, Saqqara, Egypt.

22 Akhnaton and Sun God; Egyptian Museum, Cairo.

23 Ramesseum; west bank, Luxor, Egypt.

24 (top) Temple; west bank, Luxor, Egypt.

24 (bottom) Temple columns with Ramses II; Luxor, Egypt.

25 Ramses II; Luxor, Egypt.

26 Colossi of Memnon; west bank, Luxor, Egypt.

27 Column detail, Temple of Amun; Karnak, Egypt.

27 Nefertari; Karnak, Egypt.

28 Hypostyle Hall, Temple of Amun; Karnak, Egypt.

29 Avenue of Rams; Karnak, Egypt.

30 Ruins; Bubastis, Egypt.

31 Osiris, half buried; near Aswan, Egypt.

32 Ceremonial dance; Egyptian Museum, Cairo.

32 Crocodile painting; tomb, west bank, Luxor, Egypt.

33 Sculpture of cat; Egyptian Museum, Cairo.

33 Hippopotamus; zoological garden, Cairo.

34 A physician; Egyptian Museum, Cairo.

35 Embalming symbolized on a tomb; west bank, Luxor, Egypt.

36 Lotus; botanical garden, Cairo.

36 Papyrus; botanical garden, Cairo.

37 Ancient Nile boat; Egyptian Museum, Cairo.

39 Valley of Tombs; west bank, Luxor, Egypt.

40–41 Sphinx; Giza, Egypt.

41 Step Pyramid; Saqqara, Egypt.

42 Supposed pyramid of Cheops' daughter; Giza, Egypt.

43 King Sebacus; Egyptian Museum, Cairo.

43 Amasis' Temple; Mendes, Delta, Egypt.

44 Labyrinth Pyramid; Fayum, Egypt.

45 Playing field; Olympia, Greece.

45 Landscape; near Olympia, Greece.

48 Ramses II making offering to Apis; Egyptian Museum, Cairo.

51 A Persian guard, Xerxes Palace, Persepolis; Boston Museum of Fine Arts.

52 Bull, relief, Xerxes Palace, Persepolis; Boston Museum of Fine Arts.

54 The Acropolis; Athens.

56 Hephaestus' Temple; Athens.

57 The Parthenon; Athens.

57 Acropolis from Hephaestus' Temple; Athens.

58 The Charioteer; Delphi Museum, Greece.

59 A chariot race; National Museum, Athens.

60 Mt. Athos; near Salonika, Greece.

61 Militiades' helmet; Olympia Museum, Olympia, Greece.

62 Original wall with Mt. Taygetus, Sparta, Greece.

63 Marathon beach; Marathon, Greece.

64 Marathon battlefield; Marathon, Greece.

66 Temple of Poseidon; Sunium, Greece.

68 Apollo and a centaur; Olympia Museum, Greece.

70 Achaemenid gold coin; American Numismatic Society, New York.

71 Persian gold rhyton; Metropolitan Museum of Art, New York.

72 Ramses II holding a European, Semite and Ethiopian; Egyptian Museum, Cairo.

73 Mt. Olympus, Greece.

74 The Propylaea; Acropolis, Athens.

77 Rocky Athos shore; Mt. Athos, Greece.

79 Mt. Olympus; Platamon, Greece.

80–81 Valley of Olives; Delphi, Greece.

83 Ancient olive tree; Delphi, Greece.

85 Temple of Apollo; Delphi, Greece.

86–87 Salamis Island; Greece.

88 Head of Zeus; National Museum, Athens.

89 Peneus River, Tempe Valley; south of Mt. Olympus, Greece.

92 Ancient hot springs; Thermopylae, Greece.

93 Phocian wall above Thermopylae, Greece.

94–95 Trachian cliffs; near Thermopylae, Greece.

Page

96 Leonidas; Sparta Museum, Greece.

99 Lekythos of athlete fixing his hair; Agora Museum, Athens.

101 Asopus river gorge; near Thermopylae, Greece.

102 Where Leonidas died; Thermopylae, Greece.

103 Lion of Cythera; National Museum, Athens.

104–105 Cape Artemesium, Greece.

107 Temple of Zeus; Olympia, Greece.

110 Temple of Athena Pronaea; near Delphi, Greece.

111 Snake; Acropolis Museum, Athens.

112 Athenian Treasury; Delphi, Greece.

113 Castalia spring, Delphi, Greece.

115 Temple of Apollo and Acrocorinth; Corinth, Greece.

116 Acropolis olive tree; Acropolis, Athens.

119 Temple of Aphaea; Aegina, Greece.

120 Poseidon; National Museum, Athens.

Page

123 A trireme; Acropolis Museum, Athens.

124–125 Straits of Salamis; Greece.

127 Temple of Aphaea; Aegina, Greece.

128 Alpheos River; near Olympia, Greece.

129 Themistocles ostracism sherds; American School of Classical Studies, Athens.

134 Running hoplite; Acropolis Museum, Athens.

137 Plataea battlefield; south of Thebes, Greece.

140–141 Gargaphian Spring; Plataea battleground, Greece.

141 Plataea monument base; Delphi, Greece.

143 Demeter group Eleusis; National Museum, Athens.

144 Darius gold bowl; Metropolitan Museum of Art, New York.

145 Miltiades' and Persian soldier's helmets; Olympia Museum, Greece.

INDEX

Italic numbers refer to illustrations.

Acanthus, Greece, 59, 76
Achaea, Greece, 89, 91, 92, 109
Acropolis, Athens, Greece, *54, 55, 56, 57, 74,* 84, 111, 114, *116*
Aeacus of Aegina, 58, 118, 123
Aegean islands, Greece, vii, 59
Aegila island, Greece, 61, 67
Aegina island, Greece, 59, 88, 89, 97, 106, 111, 117, 118, *119,* 122–123, 127
Aeginetans, 121, 126, 142, 145
Aeolians, 47, 72
Ajax, son of Telamon, 58, 118
Alexander I of Macedonia, 90, 131–133, 136–138
Amasis of Egypt, 45, 47
Anaxandrides, son of Leon, 97, 121, 142
Andros island, Greece, 118, 130
Arabian Gulf, 15, 38
Arabians, 17, 53, 91
Arcadia, Greece, 96, 108, 121
Argos, Greece, *x,* 1, 5–8, *6–7,* 133–134
army, Greek, 59–60, *61,* 63–65, 73–75, 78–82, 89–91, 96–103, 133–142, *134, 147*
army, Persian, *51,* 59, 72–73, 76–84, 89–92, 97–103, 106, 108, 109–118, 128–129, 131, 133–142, *147*
Artabanus, son of Hystaspes, 73–75, 78, 114
Artabazus (Persian), 136, 139, 142
Artaphernes (Persian), 71, 75
Artemisia of Halicarnassus and Cos, 118–121, 129
Artemisium, Cape, Greece, viii, 91, 100, *104–105,* 106–108, 111, 118, 122, 123
Asia, 4, 9, 38, 53, 72, 75, 76, 89–91, 138
Asopus River, Greece, 99–100, *101,* 135, 136, 139
Assyrians, 1, 17, 72
Astyages of Media, 8–10, 70
Athene (goddess), 16, 29, 55, 109–111, *110,* 114
Athens, Greece, vii, 4, *54,* 55, 59–61, 63–67, 71, 73–75, *74,* 84–87, 89, 97, 107, 108, 111–114, *116,* 118, 121, 126, 127, 129, 131–135, 139
Athos, Mt., Greece, 59, 60, 76, 77, 82
Atossa, daughter of Cyrus, 53, 69, 70, 78
Attica, Greece, 59, 87, 111–114, 126, 133–135

Bacis (Greek), 122, 126, 136
Biton of Argos, 4, 5–8
Boeotia, Greece, 55, 96, 109, 111, 113, 118, 133, 135, 138
Bottiaeis, Greece, 82, 91
Brygi (Thracians), 59, 91
Bubastis, Egypt, 29, 30, *30*
Buto, Egypt, 29, 30

calendars, 11, 49

Cambyses I of Persia (son of Teispes), 9, 75
Cambyses II of Persia, 10, 11, 47–49, 53, 69, 70
Carystus, Greece, 118, 130
Ceos island, Greece, 106, 122
Chalcis, Greece, 55, 91, 106
Chersonese peninsula, Greece, 55, 61, 76
Cilicians, 120, 128
Cimon, son of Steosagoras, 55, 60–61
Cleombrotus, son of Anaxandrides, 97, 121, 133, 142
Corinth, Greece, 96, 106, 108, *115,* 117, 121, 122
Croesus of Lydia, 2, 4, 8
Cyprians, 120, 128
Cyrene, N. Africa, vii, 37, 46
Cyrus of Persia, 9–10, 47, 48, 53, 69, 70, 75
Cythera island, Greece, 103–106, *103*

Darius of Persia, 38, 49–53, 59, 69–71, 73, 75, 76, 78, 102
Datis (Persian), 71, 75
Delphi, Greece, 4, 8, 55, 58, *80–81, 83,* 84, *85,* 109–111, *110, 112, 113,* 123, 131, 136, 145
Demaratus, son of Ariston, 69–70, 78, 82, 98, 103–106
Demeter (goddess), 29, 142, *144*
Dorians, 72, 78, 118, 132

Egypt, vii, viii, 1, 11–46, 47, 53, 69–70, 120, 128
Elephantine island (Aswan), Egypt, vii, 16, *16,* 17, 31
Eleusis, Greece, 135, 142
Elis, Greece, 44–46, *121*
Ephesus (Turkey), 44, 129
Ephialtes, son of Eurydemus, 99, 100, 102
Epidaurus, Greece, 106, 121
Eretria, Greece, 8, 59, 61, 67, 106
Ethiopia, 16, 38, 41, 72, *72*
Euboea island, Greece, 118, 121
Euripus Strait, Greece, 89, 118
Europe, 38, 70, 71, 73, 90, 91, 126
Eurybiades, son of Eurycleides, 106–107, 111, 117–118, 121, 122

Gobryas (Persian), 48–49, 69, 70, 78
Greece, viii, 1, 11, 16, 23, 29, 34, 44–46, 47, 69–71, 72, 73, 75, 76, 78, 82–84, 91, 106, 126–129, 138, 139. *See also* army; navy

Hegesistratus (Persian?), 136
Heliopolis, Egypt, 11, 15, 29
Hellespont Strait (Dardanelles, Turkey), 71, 73, 90, 114, 126, 130
Histiaea, Greece, 108, 118
Hydarnes (Persian), 49, 78
Hydarnes, son of Hydarnes, 78, 98, 99
Hystaspes, son of Arsames, 49, 69, 73, 75

Ionians, 10, 47, 72, 126
Isthmus of Corinth, Greece, 90, 97, 106, 111–118, 121, 122, 133, 135, 145

Lacedaemonians (Spartans), 97, 103–107, 126, 132, 134, 135, 138, 139, 142
Leonidas, son of Anaxandrides, *96*, 97, 100–103, 106, 108, 121, 142–144
Libya, viii, 15, 16, 30, 38, 91
Locris, Greece, 96, 97, 100, 106, 109, 118
Lydia (Turkey), viii, 2–4

Macedonia (Greece), 59, 82, 89–90, 91, 136
Magi (Persian priests), 9, 47–51, 76
Magnesia, Greece, 91, 100
Malis, Greece, 92–96, 99, 118
Marathon, Greece, viii, 59, 61, *63*, *64*, 65–67, 69
Mardonius, son of Gobryas, 59, 70, 72–75, 78, 108, 118, 126–129, 131–145
marriage, 34
Masistes, son of Darius, 78, 136
Media (Persia), 9, 48, 70, 76, 91, 98
Megabyzus (Persian), 49, 50, 76
Megara, Greece, 106, 117, 121, 133
Memphis, Egypt, 11, 12, 15, 38
Miltiades, son of Cimon, 55, 60, *61*, 63–65, *145*
Miltiades, son of Cypselus, 55–59, 61
Min of Egypt, 11, 38
Mycerinus of Egypt, *14*, 42

navy, Greek, 88, 91, 106–108, 111, 114–118, 122–126, *123*, 130
navy, Persian, 59, 67, 82, 91, 100, 103–108, 118, 126, 129–130
Nile River, Egypt, 11, 15–17, 37–38, 41

Olympia, Greece, *i*, *45*, 60, *107*, 145
Olympic Games, 44–46, 58, 60, 97, 99, 108, 121
Olympus, Mt., Greece, *73*, *79*, 82, 89, 90
Opus, Greece, 96, 97, 106
Otanes, son of Pharnaspes, 48–51, 53, 78

Papremis, Egypt, 29, 31
Pausanias, son of Cleombrotus, 133–145
Peloponnese peninsula, Greece, vii, 8, 71, 96, 97, 106, 111–121, 122, 128, 129, 132
Persia, viii, 1, *3*, 17, 38, 47–49, 51, *51*, 53, 59–61, 65–67, 69–71, 91, 98, 100, 114, 118, 129, 131, 132, 133, 135, 138–139, 142. *See also* army; navy
Phaideme, daughter of Otanes, 48, *53*
Phalerum, Greece, 67, 118, 126, 130
Phocis, Greece, 55, 91, *93*, 96, 97, 99, 100

Phoenicia, vii, 1, 118, 126, 128
Pisistratus, son of Hippocrates, 8, 55, 58, 60
Plataea, Greece, viii, 65, 106, 113–114, 118, 133, 135, 136, *137*, 139, *140–141*, 142
priests, *see* Magi; religion
pyramids, Egyptian, *13*, *14*, 38–42, *41*, *42*, 44

religion, 11, 15, 20–21, 23–30, 32, 38, 42, 47, 84, 97, 109, 121, 133

Sacae (Persians), 65, 72, 91
Sais, Egypt, 16, 46
Salamis Island, Greece, viii, 84–87, *86–87*, 111–118, 121–126, *127*, 131, 135
Samos island, Greece, vii, 44
Sane, Greece, 76, 82
Sardis (Turkey), vii, 4, 69, 71, 75, 89
Scythia (Russia), viii, 8, 16, 38, 73, 76
Sebacos of Ethiopia, 43, *43*
Sepias, Greece, 91–92, 118
Sesostris (Ramses II) of Egypt, *25*, 38, *48*, 72
Sicily, vii, 89, 107
Sicyon, Greece, 106, 121
Sparta, Greece, 1, 55, 61, 62, 67, 69, 71, 75, 78, 82, 90, 96, 98, 100, 103, 106, 107, 121, 132–135, 138, 139, 142, 145
Styra, Greece, 61, 106
Sunium, Greece, 66, 67, 131
Susa, Persia, 49, 69, 114
Syene, Egypt, 16, *17*

Tegeans, 139, 142
Tempe Valley, Greece, 89–91, *89*
Tenians (Greeks), 118, 123
Thebans, 97, 100, 102, 113, 133, 135
Thebes, Egypt, 11, 16, 31
Thebes, Greece, 8, 96, 135, 136
Themistocles, son of Neocles, 86–88, 90, 114–118, 121–123, *129*, 130
Thermopylae Pass, Greece, viii, 91–92, *92–95*, 96, 98–103, *101*, *102*, 108, 118, 121, 142, 144
Thespia, Greece, 96, 100, 113, 118, 121
Thessaly, Greece, 82, 89–90, 92, 97, 131, 133
Thrace (Balkans), 38, 55, 59, 76, 91
Torone, Greece, 76, 82
Trachis, Cliffs of, Greece, 91, *94–95*, 96, 100, 108, 118
Tritantaechmes, son of Artabanus, 78, 108
Troezen, Greece, 106, 111, 121
Troy (Turkey), 1, 76

Xerxes of Persia, 69–82, 89–90, 91–106, 108, 113–114, 118–121, 126–133, 142, 145

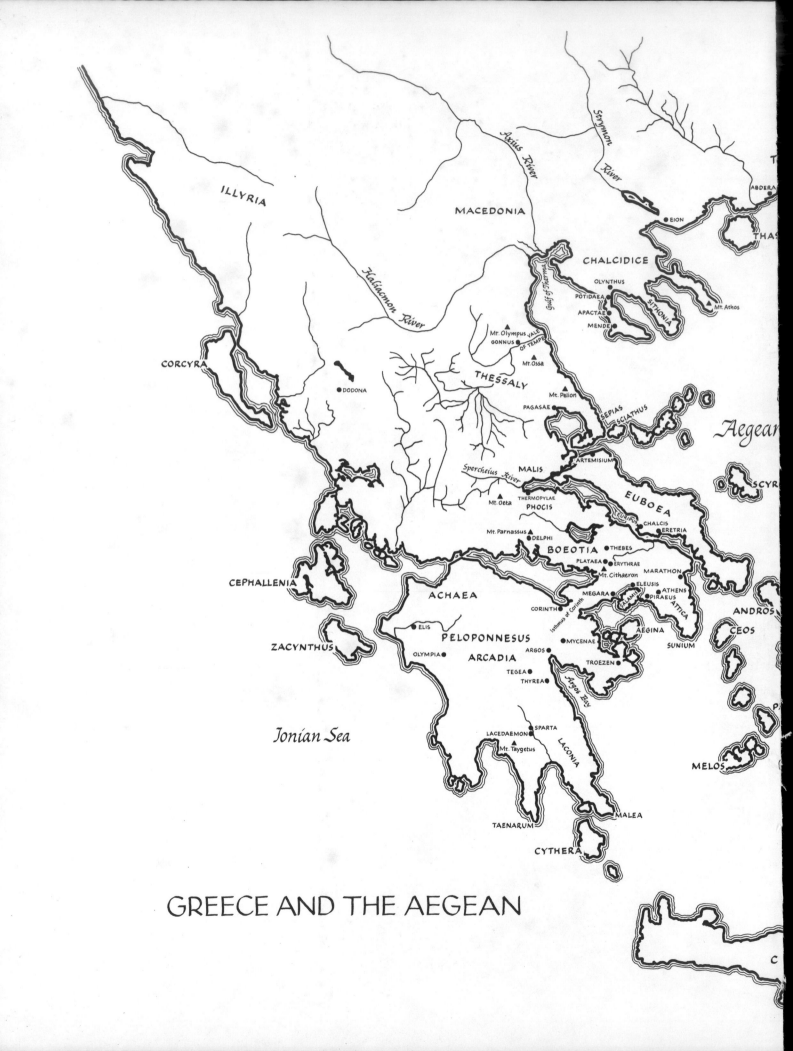

GREECE AND THE AEGEAN